EPIC ATHLETES
TOM BRADY

Dan Wetzel

Illustrations by Kazimir Lee Iskander

Henry Holt and Company

New York

For Drew Baranowski,

a Michigan man and TB12's No. 1 fan

HENRY HOLT AND COMPANY, *Publishers since 1866*
Henry Holt® is a registered trademark of Macmillan Publishing Group, LLC
120 Broadway, New York, NY 10271 • mackids.com

Library of Congress Cataloging-in-Publication Data
Names: Wetzel, Dan, author.
Title: Epic athletes : Tom Brady / Dan Wetzel.
Other titles: Tom Brady
Description: First edition. | New York : Henry Holt and Company, [2019] |
Series: Epic athletes | Audience: 008–012.
Identifiers: LCCN 2018039235 | ISBN 9781250295798 (hardcover) |
ISBN 9781250295873 (e-book)
Subjects: LCSH: Brady, Tom, 1977– —Juvenile literature. | Football players—
United States—Biography—Juvenile literature. | Quarterbacks (Football)—
United States—Biography—Juvenile literature.
Classification: LCC GV939.B685 W483 2019 | DDC 796.332092 [B]—dc23
LC record available at https://lccn.loc.gov/2018039235

Our books may be purchased in bulk for promotional, educational, or business use.
Please contact your local bookseller or the Macmillan Corporate
and Premium Sales Department at (800) 221-7945 ext. 5442 or
by email at MacmillanSpecialMarkets@macmillan.com.

First edition, 2019 / Designed by Elynn Cohen

Printed in the United States of America
by LSC Communications, Harrisonburg, Virginia
1 3 5 7 9 10 8 6 4 2

1

The Comeback

TOM BRADY WAS SPRAWLED OUT on his stomach, lying across the turf of NRG Stadium in Houston, Texas. He was looking up and watching as an Atlanta Falcons cornerback named Robert Alford sprinted through the open field toward a touchdown in the Super Bowl.

Just moments earlier, Brady tried to complete a pass to wide receiver Danny Amendola, when Alford stepped in front of him, intercepted the ball, raced to his right, avoided Brady's leaping tackle, and then took it all the way for a touchdown, a pick-six. After winding up in a heap on the field, Brady could do nothing but watch. High above, in the second quarter of the Super Bowl in February of 2017, the scoreboard read Atlanta 21, New England 0. No team had ever trailed by more than ten points and won the Big Game.

Tom Brady and the Patriots were in big, big trouble.

By the middle of the third quarter, it was even worse, Atlanta leading 28–3. All around the world people began turning off their televisions and giving up on New England. The Patriots had won four Super Bowls with Tom as their quarterback. They had executed dozens of miraculous comebacks across his long career, but this felt like too much even for the veteran QB.

Yet down on the Patriots sideline one person had most certainly not given up: Tom Brady. Tom began walking along the team bench shouting at his teammates to ignore the scoreboard and "just do your job!" They quickly cut the lead to 28–9. He told them to forget the dwindling time on the clock and "worry about the next play." Soon it was 28–12. He reminded them to "trust the process" and keep going. Suddenly it was 28–20. Tom kept screaming "come on, come on!" Now it was Atlanta's sideline that was nervous, scared they might blow the big lead in the Big Game.

By the time New England running back James White scored a touchdown and Tom passed it to Amendola for a two-point conversion, tying the score at 28–28 with fifty-seven seconds remaining, he didn't have to say anything.

"You just looked in his eyes," receiver Matthew Slater said.

If there ever was a football star who would not panic in the face of a 28–3 second-half deficit against a team as good as Atlanta, who wouldn't point fingers at failure but instead try to rally everyone together, who wouldn't be overcome by doubt, but instead recommit to the game plan, it would be Tom Brady. In one dramatic comeback, by far the largest in Super Bowl history, Tom relived his entire career. He'd never listened to anyone who counted him out.

Tom grew up in San Mateo, California, near San Francisco, the youngest child of four, with three very athletic sisters. He spent much of his youth trying to prove he could play with the older girls—softball, soccer, basketball, whatever was being played at his family's home. He was an excellent quarterback at Junipero Serra High School, but when he arrived at the University of Michigan, he didn't see much playing time during his first three years on campus. He considered transferring back to a college in California, but he didn't like the idea of quitting. Instead he decided to stick it out and fight for the starting spot. He still didn't fully win the job until the second half of his senior year.

Given his limited college success, almost no one thought he'd be much of a National Football League (NFL) player. New England drafted him in the sixth round, 199th overall. NFL teams drafted six other quarterbacks ahead of him. Tom wasn't sure he'd even make any team, and he began thinking about a career outside of football. He barely played as a rookie, but he kept plugging away, improving his mechanics, studying game film, and preparing each week like he was the starter even though he mostly just stood on the sideline and held a clipboard.

In 2001, his second season, he only got in on the action because the starter was injured. Fans thought Tom would be a temporary fill-in. Tom saw things differently. Finally, here was his big chance.

He led New England to a victory in his first start, then they won four of five, and then finished the year with six consecutive victories. Each week he seemed to get a little better, a little more comfortable, a little more confident. The Patriots plowed through the playoffs and got into the Super Bowl, where they were a huge underdog to the defending champion Saint Louis Rams. Few believed in them, but Tom led a final-minute game-winning drive. The unheralded quarterback was the champion no one saw coming. He was just twenty-four years old.

By the time Super Bowl LI vs. Atlanta came along fifteen years later, Brady was considered perhaps the greatest quarterback ever. He'd been named Most Valuable Player (MVP) twice. His name was written all over the record books. He'd become a superstar. Yet he had never lost that initial fire, that drive, that sense that the world didn't believe in him. Sticking with the plan and never giving up hope—even in the face of long odds—is how he got to that point. It's why he kept telling his teammates the game wasn't over, no matter the score.

"You just have to keep going," Tom said.

His teammates listened intently because they had grown up watching Tom Brady become a legend. Wide receiver Chris Hogan was thirteen in February of 2002 when Brady and the Patriots beat Saint

Louis for that first Super Bowl title. Hogan watched the game in his living room in New Jersey at his family's annual Super Bowl party. Tight end Matt Lengel was eleven at the time, watching with his grandfather in Kentucky. Special teamer Matthew Slater was with his brother in Southern California. Running back James White was ten in Florida. Receiver Malcolm Mitchell was nine in Georgia.

These are the kids Brady inspired to play football. These are the kids who grew up watching him do the impossible and then went out in their backyards and dreamed of being him. Now they could hardly believe they shared a locker room and a huddle with him, suddenly starring in their own boyhood dreams.

"When Tom Brady says it, you listen," Mitchell said.

"I believed it the entire time," Hogan said. "He gave us the kick. He got everyone fired up."

The comeback was achieved one play at a time. One run. One pass. One block. One tackle. One field goal. Tom kept reminding his teammates that if everyone kept pulling in the same direction, then anything was possible. It's how Tom built his career. He isn't the biggest, the fastest, the strongest, or the most talented player in the world. He may be the most determined. He learned that while winning was great, the joy was in the journey and the daily challenges of practice and workouts when no one is watching and you are only competing against yourself. If he wasn't like that, he probably would have quit football at Michigan and never been heard of in the world of sports again.

There was another reason, a special reason, Tom was so intent on making his teammates keep playing hard. This was his seventh Super Bowl, but it was the first time in over a year that his mother, Galynn, had been able to come to a game and watch him play football. She had been stricken with cancer and had spent the previous months in her own daily battle against giving up, this one involving chemotherapy and recovery, doctors and hospitals.

Galynn was in California fighting. Tom was in Massachusetts working. Despite all his fortune and fame, there were times he felt helpless, a son unable to protect his mother. Tom didn't know if she would even make it to the Super Bowl. He certainly didn't know how many more games his seventy-two-year-old mother would ever see. He wasn't going to give up now.

"We talked at his locker before the game," Patriots owner Robert Kraft said. "This is the first game his mother had been at. She'd been going through a lot. And he said, 'Let's win . . . this one is for her.' And I was thinking when we were down, when it was 28–3, how he must have felt."

In overtime, New England won the toss and got the ball, first and ten on their own twenty-five-yard line. A touchdown would win it. Tom hit White for six yards, then Amendola for fourteen, and Hogan for eighteen. Just like that, the Pats were at the Atlanta thirty-seven. They kept on rolling. Next came another completion to White, followed by a fifteen-yard pass to Julian Edelman, and then a White ten-yard run pushed the Pats within striking distance of the end zone. A penalty moved the ball to the Atlanta two-yard line. The Falcons defense was exhausted, flustered, and unsure what Tom Brady was going to hit them with next.

"It was just an avalanche on them," Brady said.

Finally, Tom pitched the ball to White, who barreled in for the touchdown, New England 34, Atlanta 28. Miraculously, they had secured the comeback and another championship was won.

Tom finished the game with 466 yards passing and two touchdowns. He completed an amazing twenty-six of thirty-four passes for 284 yards and two touchdowns in his final five drives, when the comeback took shape. He was five of six in over-time. He even scrambled for fifteen yards and a critical first down. It was Tom at his best.

When it was over, as his teammates hugged and jumped around, Tom fell to the field and put his head down and cried, his tears falling with the celebratory confetti. He'd taken a physical beating—five sacks and so many more hits. He'd been drained emotionally; belief in the face of doubt is sapping.

In postgame chaos, Galynn was hustled out onto the field, surrounded by family, overcome with joy to see her son. "Unbelievable," she said. Soon her husband, Tom Sr., was crying, too. So were Tom's sisters. Tom's wife and kids were there, offering up kisses to their dad. Tom was fine with the tears and smiles. "I wear my emotions on my jersey sleeve," Brady said. "I've got my family here. A lot of emotion." He doesn't worry about looking cool.

Robert Kraft could only marvel once again at the unlikely draft pick who had become among the greatest the game had ever seen.

"The greater the pressure," the Patriots owner said, "the better he performs."

2

Growing Up

THOMAS EDWARD PATRICK BRADY JR. was born on August 3, 1977. He was named after his father, Tom Sr., who along with mother Galynn was thrilled to bring a fourth child into the world, if for nothing else because he was a boy. Tom's three older siblings were all girls. The oldest, Maureen, was then four and the youngest, Nancy, was sixteen months old. Then there was Julie, the middle sister, who coincidentally turned three that very day. Since Tom and Julie share a birthday, they jokingly call each other "twins" even though they were born three years apart.

The Bradys lived on a quiet street in San Mateo, California, a suburb just south of San Francisco. The weather there is great almost the entire year and Tom Sr., who ran his own insurance firm, and Galynn, who was a flight attendant before concentrating on raising her children, believed in an active, outdoor lifestyle. Whether it was in the backyard, out in the street in front of their home, or even in the living room, games were played nonstop, competition relentless between the three sisters and their kid brother.

Growing up, the family spent their weekends running from one game to the next, and their weeknights shuttling from one practice to another. Tom recalls his dad always finding time for him, even if it was just hitting some fly balls at night when he returned from work, or going to a local driving range to practice golf. Tom played whatever sport was in season, either on city recreational teams or through the Catholic Youth Organization (CYO) teams at his school, Saint Gregory's Catholic School, which he attended from kindergarten through eighth grade.

"It was just great to grow up in a house like that

and feel so supported by your mom and dad," Tom said. "I've always had that great support at home. I certainly wouldn't be [in the NFL] if I didn't have the love and support of my parents and my sisters and my family."

The Bradys are a devout Catholic family, and growing up, Tom served as an altar boy at his local parish on Sundays. Tom Sr. also wanted him to have a job as a kid so he would learn the value of work and begin to understand how to manage money. Tom soon delivered newspapers around San Mateo, sometimes with his mother driving him while Tom showed off his future football arm by chucking papers out the window and landing them on people's doorsteps. Both of his parents were strict with discipline and grades, making all their kids keep their studies up in order to play games. As good as all the kids were at sports, no one expected any of them to make a living doing it. There was fun and there was school. There was never a doubt which was more important.

Tom found there were benefits in being the only boy in a family of sisters. "It was great. I didn't have anyone to share clothes with. I didn't have to fight over the bathroom," Tom said. "They were pretty easy on me. They'd bring all of their girlfriends over to the house. It was pretty cool."

Tom played just about everything as a kid—baseball, soccer, basketball, golf—you name it. Except he never played football. While he would sometimes play unorganized games for fun with his friends, Tom didn't take up competitive football until he reached high school. Before that he was considered an excellent all-around athlete, especially in Little League baseball. What drove him was trying to keep up with his sisters, who were older, bigger, and better. They'd compete over everything, not just sports but board games, card games, grades, even who controlled the TV remote.

"They were the best athletes in my house," Tom said. "They were certainly better athletes than me. They all had successful athletic careers. It was a very athletic family. We grew up on baseball and soccer fields. I loved just tagging along. I loved going out there and cheering them on. I was living and dying with every win and loss that they had."

Maureen was a softball star who threw sixty-nine shutouts, twenty-nine no-hitters, and fourteen perfect games in high school. She also played for the US Junior Olympic team and was an All-American at California State University, Fresno. Whenever

Tom joined a new team in the city or made a good play in a game—whether it was making a basket or hitting a home run—people would point and say, "That's Maureen Brady's little brother."

Julie was an incredible soccer player who earned a scholarship to Saint Mary's College of California. Meanwhile, Nancy followed Maureen into softball and was offered a full scholarship to the University of California, Berkeley. Tom later realized that by not getting all the attention in his house, it helped him develop the determination to get better. Still, he yearned for the day when he would simply be known as "Tom Brady," or maybe even when Maureen would be known as "Tom Brady's older sister." In elementary school, he once told his mother that "one day I'm going to be a household name." She laughed.

Having that many great athletes in one family is almost unheard of, but for the Bradys it seemed normal. Galynn, their mother, was herself a gifted athlete, especially in soccer. Unfortunately, she grew up in an era when there were limited opportunities for female athletes. Even into her forties, however, she routinely beat her children at tennis, took up golf, and still found time to play in competitive soccer leagues in the Bay Area.

Tom was a standout golfer as a kid and some wonder if he couldn't have turned pro in that sport had he devoted the time to it. The thing about golf is that it requires endless practice to refine the smallest of skills. You have to spend hours repeating the same shot. Tom was a multisport athlete and wasn't willing to give up on everything else just for golf. He remains a strong although far from professional level golfer, though. He enjoys playing with his dad more than anyone.

But of all the sports he played as a kid, Tom really excelled in baseball. He was obsessed with the sport. "I loved baseball," Tom said. He collected boxes of baseball cards and played on as many Little League teams as he could. San Mateo and the surrounding areas were considered baseball country, producing a lot of great talent. Tom attended San Mateo's Junipero Serra High School, an all-boys Catholic high school, about a decade behind Barry Bonds, who would go on to hit more home runs (762) than anyone in Major League Baseball (MLB) history. In San Mateo, anyone who thought Tom might make a name for himself as a professional athlete thought it would be in baseball.

Tom was a catcher. He threw righty but batted

lefty. His arm strength, which would one day tor-ment NFL defenses, could easily cut down opponents trying to steal second base. At Serra High School, he batted .311 with enough power to regularly hit home runs. His most legendary high school homer came in a road game. The team bus was parked on the other side of the outfield wall, where the bus driver was taking a nap during the game. At least, he was sleeping until Brady hit a towering shot that cleared the fence and hit the roof of the bus, startling and waking up the driver. His teammates couldn't stop laughing from the dugout. Tom was named all-league as a senior. A number of MLB teams scouted him and worked him out as a high school senior, including the Seattle Mariners and the Montreal Expos, who are now the Washington Nationals.

One night during his senior year, Montreal was playing a game against the San Francisco Giants at Candlestick Park, which wasn't far from where the Bradys lived. The Expos invited Tom to come over and take batting practice with the team, a pseudo workout. Tom walked out onto the field and hit the ball all over the stadium. "It was an impressive workout for the young man," then Expos General

Manager Kevin Malone told Bleacher Report. "He had a pretty good swing, and he had power. He was not overwhelmed by the stadium or by hanging around major-league players. He had poise. You wouldn't know—except for looking at his young face—that this guy was not part of our major-league Montreal Expos team. He carried himself like a professional. He had that 'it' factor."

Tom was impressive, but he was also, at that point, determined to play college football (a sport he'd fallen in love with while playing on his high school team), which scared off a number of baseball teams. Had he committed to baseball, he would have been picked in the first few rounds of the MLB draft. Montreal, in particular, thought he could be its starting catcher for years to come. They liked Tom so much they picked him in the eighteenth round of the 1995 MLB draft even though he said he wouldn't sign with them. They basically wasted a pick in case college football didn't work out and he decided to return to baseball—a clear sign of how talented they thought he was.

"I think he could have been one of the greatest catchers ever," Malone said. "I know that's quite a statement, but the projections were based on the fact we had a left-hand-hitting catcher, with arm strength and who was athletic . . . But his first love was football."

We can only wonder what type of catcher Tom Brady might've become had he decided to play baseball. But thankfully for a generation of future Patriots fans, Tom Brady's football career was just beginning.

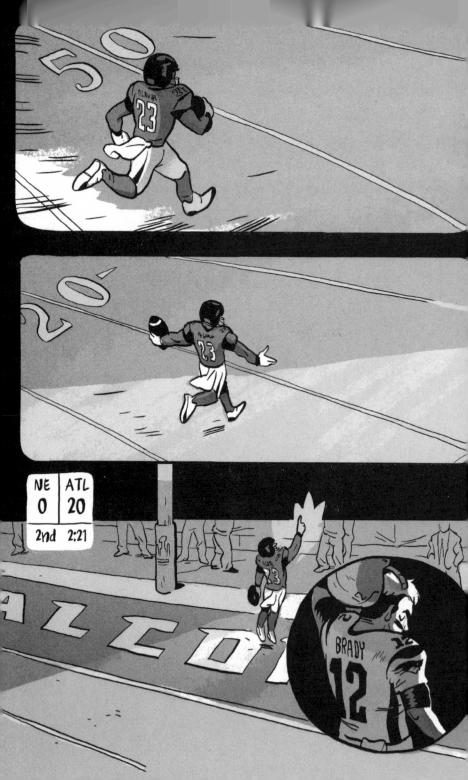

3

High School

CANDLESTICK PARK SAT about fifteen miles from the Bradys' home. It was a huge, towering stadium built in 1958 on the edge of San Francisco Bay, about halfway between the San Francisco International Airport and the city itself. The MLB Giants played there until 2000, when they moved to a new ballpark closer to downtown San Francisco. The local NFL team, the 49ers, called it home until 2013, when Levi's Stadium was finished down in Santa Clara. The weather in San Francisco is usually nice, but it can quickly be washed over by fog or light rain from the Pacific Ocean. Locals know that it is unpredictable, often joking, "If you don't like the weather, wait half an hour." Due to its placement on the edge of the bay, Candlestick became famous for swirling winds, gusts, and sometimes fog, drizzle, and cold air. That was tough enough for football. It was even worse for baseball.

To the Bradys and millions of local sports fans though, it was heaven. The family bought 49ers season tickets and held on to them for twenty-four years, basically until Tom made the NFL and they became New England Patriots fans. On game day, they would follow a simple routine: Everyone got up early for church, rushed home after services to change into 49ers shirts and jackets, then headed to the stadium to have a tailgate lunch in the parking lot, and finally went inside to watch the game. They didn't have the best seats—way back in the upper deck—but they were there among the crowd, the noise, and the energy of game day. And the games were usually really good because the 49ers were the NFL's best team at the time.

This is where Tom's love of football came from, not as a Pop Warner youth league player, but as a regular NFL fan, attending games with his family.

In 1981, when Tom was four years old, through 1998, when he was in college, the 49ers reached the playoffs sixteen of eighteen seasons and won five Super Bowls. These were the years Tom became a fan, drawn in by the team's success and seeing the sport through the best of moments. He became obsessed with the franchise's two star quarterbacks, first Joe Montana and then Steve Young, who are both in the Pro Football Hall of Fame.

"Joe Montana and Steve Young were my two favorite players," Tom said. "It was really great to grow up in the Bay Area at that time and watch two of the greatest quarterbacks to ever play. That's really where I began to love football."

Tom was present at one of the most famous NFL games ever, the 1981 National Football Conference Championship Game between San Francisco and Dallas. The Cowboys led by six late into the game, and the 49ers were running out of chances to keep their season alive. That's when the 49ers got the ball on their own eleven-yard line with 4:54 remaining. Montana began slowly driving them down the field. A first down here. A great pass there. Soon San Francisco faced a third down from the Cowboys six-yard line. Just fifty-eight seconds remained. Montana took the snap, scrambled to his right, and was pursued by three Dallas defenders. He held on for as long as he could before firing a pass into the end zone, where Dwight Clark jumped in the air and grabbed the ball with his fingertips. The 49ers won. History was made.

It was dubbed "The Catch" and began the 49ers' run of dominance. Four-year-old Tom cheered wildly in the stands like all the other San Francisco fans. The day wasn't all great, though. Tom previously had been upset and cried because he wanted his dad to buy him an oversized 49ers No. 1 foam finger. He was just a little kid, and even one of the best games ever couldn't hold his attention for three full hours. He remembers the great players and games, but he really treasures the time he spent with his family that taught him to love not just the sport of football, but everything that surrounds it.

"To have a chance to go to the 49ers game with my dad and my mom and throw the ball in the parking lot before the games, those are memories that I'll have forever," Tom said. "It was always a special time for me. We'd sit down in the end zone about ten rows from the top of the stadium in

Candlestick, which is the greatest field to begin with, and watch a lot of great 49ers games."

When the 49ers won the Super Bowl, his mother would take all the kids out of school and drive them down to see the championship parade in San Francisco. They'd draw handmade signs and bring along pots and spoons to clank and make a lot of noise. Tom would scream and cheer as his favorite players rolled by in the backs of trucks or in convertibles, waving to the thousands of fans crowding the sidewalks.

When Tom entered Serra High School, he decided he wanted to play football in addition to baseball and some golf on the side. There are some sports that require a great deal of practice and precise training at an early age in order to excel—golf, tennis, gymnastics, even soccer and basketball. You can't just pick those up at fourteen or fifteen years old and expect to be competitive at a high level. For example, Simone Biles, the great Olympic gold medalist in gymnastics, began training competitively at the age of six, devoting nearly all her free time to the sport. Some gymnasts start even younger than that.

But football is different and is often a sport that really works for multisport athletes or kids who have later growth spurts. While youth football is fun and can help develop talent, it isn't a requirement for being a good high school, college, or even NFL player. Players can get serious at a later age and develop very quickly. Oftentimes, being an all-around athlete is the best preparation for being a football player.

When Tom went out for his freshman team, he wanted to be a quarterback like Joe Montana, who had at that point led the 49ers to four Super Bowls and twice been named NFL MVP. Because of baseball, Tom knew he had a strong arm, and he often played quarterback in neighborhood games. He thought he could toss the ball pretty well. The problem was, just about every kid in the San Francisco Bay Area wanted to be Joe Montana.

Eight guys tried out for quarterback on the freshman team alone. None of them looked very skilled. Tom really just wanted to play, so he was willing to try any position. Freshman football is often that way—kids playing both sides of the ball, offense and defense, and testing out new spots to see what they are good at. The coaches already had a more polished quarterback, Kevin Krystofiak, who would be the starter. So Tom decided to try his hand at defense and began practicing some at linebacker.

He was known as a big hitter and someone who craved the contact that can make the game fun. He tried to learn to be a quarterback in practice, but he was still very raw.

It wasn't just Tom Brady who needed work. The entire Junipero Serra freshman team struggled. Everyone was still learning and trying to come together as a team. They didn't win a single game that season, finishing 0–8–1. Serra often got blown out. The team struggled so much that it scored a measly *two* offensive touchdowns the entire season. No one who coached, watched, or played could have predicted that one of the greatest football players of all time was on the roster.

Being on the bench of a losing team was a good lesson for Tom, a better one, he thinks, than if he'd had instant success. He realized you can't just show up and excel, which taught him the value of dedication and practice. He came to understand that football is the ultimate team game; you need all eleven players on the field to contribute on each play or your team doesn't stand a chance. And he knew that if he didn't put in some work to get better, he'd never see the field.

During the summer before his sophomore

season, he began putting himself through individual workouts, trying to improve his throwing accuracy and his footwork. They included everything from lifting weights to jumping rope. One training routine he learned was called the "five-dot drill." The coaches would put down five cones or "dots" on the field, laid out in a two-one-two pattern, just like the dots on the five side of a die. They then had their players run through patterns, touching all five spots, faster and faster as the drill sped up. It was boring and tiring and improvement came very slowly, so most players hated it.

Tom was different. He became obsessed with it. Kevin Krystofiak had told Tom he wasn't coming back for junior varsity football. Kevin was going to concentrate on basketball, which was his best sport. The starting quarterback job was open and Tom wanted it. The only way he knew to get it was to get better. He didn't just do the five-dot drill at practice, he did it all the time. He drew the five dots on the family patio in the backyard and ran through it until he was exhausted. It didn't matter if he was alone or had a friend over or the family invited company for a cookout. There was Tom, practicing the five-dot drill. Sometimes he'd get up early and do it a few times before school. He did it all spring and all summer. He needed to put in the work, describing himself as a "slow, chubby sophomore."

Tom was growing into a big kid entering his sophomore year, standing at six foot three and weighing 205 pounds. Yet he was a bit clumsy, still waiting for his agility to catch up. The five-dot drill helped him bridge that gap. As he walked into practice before his sophomore season, the kid who couldn't play quarterback for a winless team his freshman year looked like a potential star.

"Over the summer, it was like someone flipped a switch," Tom's old teammate John Kirby once told the *New York Daily News*. "You could tell he had a chance to be something special."

Tom became the starter on the junior varsity team and things were immediately different. In the season opener, Serra trailed San Jose Mission High School by five points with about two minutes remaining. That's when, for the first time, Tom did something he became famous for doing. He gathered the team in the huddle, and with a calm but purposeful voice said they had to come together and win the game. The guys listened. The blocking was strong. The wide receivers ran perfect routes. And

Tom delivered the ball, one completion after the next. In the end, he hit Kirby in the end zone with less than thirty seconds remaining.

Serra won the game. The kids on Serra, most who like Tom had never won a game before, celebrated like they had captured the Super Bowl. It was an exciting moment, reaffirming Tom's love for football and teamwork. Football, he thought, was the greatest game of all. It also proved to him that there is no substitute for hard work. There was no way Serra would've won if he hadn't completed all those five-dot drills when no one was watching or cheering or keeping score.

By the end of the season, Serra was in the JV league championship game against San Jose's Bellarmine College Preparatory. Trailing by six, Tom led Serra on a late, potential title-winning drive, only to have the game delayed when the field's automatic sprinklers went off. After a delay, the game resumed on a soaked field until the sprinklers went off again and Brady fumbled a wet ball. Bellarmine won. Tom and his teammates' hopes of winning a championship were dashed.

Tom will never forget the "Sprinkler Game." It is one reason why he still likes to practice using footballs that are dunked in a bucket of water just before the snap. It's designed to get him comfortable handling a soaked ball during games played in the rain or snow. And it's proved very useful in his long career. Stadium sprinklers have never gone off in the middle of a big NFL game yet, but you just never know.

Tom employed that same on-field work ethic off the field as well. He was driven in all aspects of his life. He worked hard to make good grades. He rarely stayed out late, even on the weekends. He rose early to either fit in a pre-school workout or catch up on studying. It's not that he didn't have fun; he was the same charismatic leader he is now. He was popular, but he lived life with a purpose. He wanted to be the greatest athlete he could be—both in baseball and football at that point. He also wanted to attend the best college he could in order to receive the best education possible. Being a professional athlete was not assured. He wasn't putting all his eggs in that basket. He was just trying to make the most out of high school.

As a junior, Tom was ready to be the Serra High varsity team starting quarterback. Serra was more of a baseball powerhouse than a football one, though.

By the fall of 1993, former Serra baseball star Barry Bonds had signed with the Giants and was en route to hitting forty-six home runs and winning his third MVP award in four years. Everyone at Serra was proud and excited. But the football team had spawned some greats of its own, producing Pittsburgh Steelers Hall of Fame receiver Lynn Swann. With that type of amazing athletic legacy, Tom must've felt the pressure.

Serra's main challenge was that it played in the West Catholic Athletic League, one of the strongest conferences in the entire state of California. Tom developed nicely as a starter, throwing for 3,514 yards and thirty-three touchdowns during his junior and senior year seasons. Still, despite Tom's massive improvement, his team could never dominate the conference or compete with the best teams of the day, Bellarmine and Mountain View's Saint Francis High School. Serra went 6–4 during Tom's junior year season and 5–5 as a senior.

A quarterback who would one day dominate the NFL postseason didn't qualify for the playoffs in his entire high school career.

4

Recruitment

THOUGH HE'D DEVELOPED significantly as a quarterback, Tom Brady's stats in high school weren't all that special. They were good, but plenty of other players threw for more yards and more touchdowns. His team did not have the most success. It never even won a conference title, let alone a state championship. Its record was barely above .500. Despite playing in a major suburb of a big city, Tom and the rest of the Bradys weren't sure if he would be heavily recruited to play college football because so few coaches knew about him.

Tom had the ability to play college football, but first he had to get recruiters to notice him. One of the factors holding him back was that at the time, Tom was better at baseball than football, which made him worried that schools might assume he would get drafted and go play minor-league ball. The opposite was true, though. Once Tom began playing football, that became his focus. He loved it more than baseball.

After Tom's junior year season, only one major college was recruiting him: the University of California, Berkeley. He had been to Cal's summer camp and caught the eyes of the coaches. He had a good relationship with everyone in Berkeley. It was a solid option. Cal played in what is now known as the Pac-12 Conference, was a great academic school, and with its location just across the San Francisco Bay from San Mateo, it would be easy for his family to come watch him play. The issues were football related. Cal had just four winning seasons in the previous fifteen years, didn't draw many fans, and rarely played in big, exciting, nationally televised games. Playing time might be easier to get, but Cal wasn't considered one of the major programs in the country at the time.

The Bradys wanted more options. They wanted to see who else might be interested. Tom liked Cal, but maybe he'd like somewhere else, too. His family got Tom's game film and cut up a highlight reel. The video began with Tom's high school coach, Tom MacKenzie, vouching for him. "He's a big, strong, durable athlete who definitely has an excellent work ethic, especially in the off-season, and does things to make him a Division I athlete," Coach MacKenzie said.

This was years before companies provided these kinds of services on the Internet. These days, players can put highlights up on websites like Rivals, Hudl, or YouTube and market themselves to coaches across the country. The Bradys had to make tapes and figure out which schools were worth paying the price of shipping. Tom and his father made a list of schools they were interested in, focusing first on places with strong academics. At this point, there was no guarantee Tom would play in the NFL, so he wanted to get a degree he could use in life. He also wanted to find a school that he would want to attend if football didn't work out. They made a list of fifty-four universities and sent out the tapes.

It worked. Recruiters saw a strong-armed player

with a lot of poise. His team didn't always win, but it was clear Tom Brady had potential.

A number of coaches reached out and Tom soon cut his list to three: Cal, the University of Illinois, and the University of Michigan. Tom Sr. made it no secret that he was rooting for Cal. He and Tom were close and he preferred having his son thirty-eight miles away across the Bay, rather than two thousand miles away in the Midwest. They could still visit each other and even slip away to play golf. Getting to games would be easy. And Cal needed him.

Tom decided to take a recruiting visit to Illinois, but the trip didn't excite him. He called home to say the weather was gray and cold and he was ruling out the Fighting Illini. His dad was secretly happy. He figured the weather would be similar when Tom visited Michigan.

It was, but everything else about Michigan was different. The Wolverines represented big-time college football. Michigan Stadium, which is appropriately nicknamed "The Big House," sat over one hundred thousand fans and was sold out for every game. The Wolverines' winged helmets and maize-and-blue uniforms were iconic. The fight song was legendary. They were routinely ranked in the top ten in the country and played on national television almost every week. They had a tradition of greatness, and from 1988–1992 they won at least a share of the Big Ten Championship, which resulted in four trips to the famed Rose Bowl. Michigan was also an elite academic school.

Billy Harris was an assistant coach at Michigan at the time. He was in charge of recruiting high schoolers from California for the Wolverines, and after he saw Tom's highlight tape he began calling every week. As Harris and the Bradys grew close, he soon believed that Tom would make a great quarterback at Michigan. First, though, he had to convince Head Coach Gary Moeller to offer Tom a scholarship and then make sure Tom would accept it.

Tom was a California kid and had a local option. Was he really willing to move so far from his family? Was he really willing to come all the way to Michigan, where winter blasts and piles of snow were common? Harris tried to spin the weather argument around. He told Tom that while warm temperatures were nice, if he ever made it to the NFL, having experience playing in the cold and snow of the Midwest would be a huge advantage.

Once Tom took a recruiting trip he was ready

to kiss the sunshine goodbye. Ann Arbor is a beautiful college town surrounding a vibrant campus. He met professors, fellow students, and potential future teammates. There was so much history and pride in the program, it overwhelmed him. Michigan was special. They didn't just recruit anyone, let alone someone all the way from California. There were plenty of kids from Detroit and Cleveland and Chicago eager to go there. This was a coaching staff that believed in him. And when the coaches walked Tom out of the tunnel and onto the field of massive Michigan Stadium to gaze up at the rows and rows of bleachers, it was over. Tom wanted to be a Wolverine.

"I was hoping that one day I would get a chance to lead the team onto Michigan Stadium in front of 112,000 fans," Tom said.

Back in San Mateo, he told everyone about the trip. His high school coaches, who had assumed he was headed to Cal, now figured he was locked in for Michigan. The only concern anyone had was just how committed the Wolverines were to Tom Brady. Sure, the coaches seemed to be on his side, but in sports, fortunes can change in a hot second, and just because you're the next big thing one day, doesn't mean that it will last. Plus, Michigan already had a deep group of quarterbacks in the program and would continue to add great recruits. Tom knew, unlike at Cal, he would be going in with little opportunity to play right away and wouldn't be the local kid that the fans and media already knew. Would he get a fair chance? Or would they just bring him in, and if he didn't immediately develop, recruit new players, meaning he would never play?

Harris and Head Coach Gary Moeller flew to San Mateo and met with Tom and his family in their home. They promised they saw him as the future of the program. He would have every opportunity to prove himself. No, it wouldn't be easy, but they said beating out other great players, rather than being handed a starting job, would make him better. Tom embraced it. He wanted the challenge.

Tom Sr. knew it would be heartbreaking to be so far from his son, but he also knew it was an incredible opportunity for Tom to get a world-class degree and play for one of the best teams in America. After a few more weeks of thought and discussion, Tom talked to Harris on the phone and committed. He was going to be a Wolverine.

Tom signed his national letter of intent in February of 1995, during his senior year of high school. Not long after that, Billy Harris called and broke some news to Tom—he was leaving his job as an assistant coach at Michigan to become the defensive coordinator at Stanford University, which coincidentally sits just a few miles from San Mateo but never recruited Tom. The new job was a promotion, so the Bradys understood. College football is a business. Still, it was a shock because Harris was the person on the coaching staff whom they knew the best and had developed a relationship with. He was also Tom's biggest fan in Ann Arbor, the one who presumably would push for Tom to get practice reps and playing time. Harris remained close to Tom and his family, though, even attending his going away party that summer and bringing a Michigan flag as a gift.

As if having Harris leave wasn't tough enough, in April of 1995, Gary Moeller was arrested after an incident while he was out to dinner in Southfield, Michigan. The university decided to fire him. Suddenly the head coach who saw Brady as the future was gone, too. Tom didn't know the other coaches nearly as well, especially the new head coach, Lloyd Carr, who had been promoted from defensive coordinator to replace Coach Moeller.

By the time Tom left for Ann Arbor, it was clear

he was in for a long battle to prove himself. The coaches who recruited him were out. The new ones were under pressure to win. That meant every snap, whether it was in practice or in games, was going to be fought over. And here he was, coming in from the Bay Area, an unknown kid on a stacked roster. No one was getting on the field without earning it. This was the big time he said he wanted.

If Tom thought battling his way up the depth chart would make him a better player, he couldn't have asked for better opportunity than this. The depth chart couldn't be much deeper.

"When I got to Ann Arbor, I was the seventh-string quarterback," Tom said.

5

Depth Chart

IN THE FALL OF 1995, Tom Brady took what the National Collegiate Athletic Association (NCAA) calls a "redshirt" year. It meant he was on scholarship, went to class, and participated in all of Michigan football's practices, meetings, and training sessions. He just wasn't eligible to play.

The way the rule works is this: In exchange for not playing one season, he still had four years of eligibility remaining, and would therefore be in school for five years total. It's like staying back a grade in school, just in this case it's for football. For

Tom, it made sense. By not playing, he could concentrate a bit more on his studies that first year away from home so he was on pace to earn a diploma while getting stronger, quicker, and more fundamentally sound on the field. This was a chance to trade his potentially worst season—as an eighteen-year-old true freshman—for his potentially best season—a bigger, more experienced twenty-two-year-old fifth-year senior. Had he been eligible to play his first year, he wouldn't have gotten much time on the field anyway. At Michigan, redshirting is what quarterbacks generally did. It is the way most strong football programs operate.

The following season, 1996, Tom was eligible to play, but barely did. The starting quarterback was a redshirt sophomore named Scott Dreisbach. The second-stringer was a redshirt junior named Brian Griese, the son of NFL Hall of Fame quarterback Bob Griese. Brady, now a redshirt freshman, was third string, just beating out two other quarterbacks. Practice reps were limited, but Tom did what he could to prepare himself. He put in extra work after practice to continue to improve his accuracy and tried to watch closely and learn during games.

Tom's first appearance as a college player came

in the third game of the season. Michigan was hosting University of California, Los Angeles, and led 35–3 going into the fourth quarter. With a victory all but assured, Coach Carr decided to give Tom a chance to play. On Tom's first pass attempt, he dropped back and threw the ball to his left . . . right into the arms of UCLA linebacker Phillip Ward, who intercepted it and immediately raced forty-five yards the other way for a touchdown. Tom Brady's first college pass was a pick-six.

"I was horrified," Tom said years later, making fun of himself for the error. "That was UCLA's only touchdown of the game. A forty-five-yard interception return. Welcome to college football. I wasn't sure my coach would ever put me in again."

The 1996 season wasn't much fun for Tom. He played in just two games and completed just three passes on five attempts for the season. He was incredibly discouraged. Not only were Gary Moeller and Billy Harris gone, but prior to that season, quarterbacks coach Kit Cartwright had left for a different job. Tom felt like he didn't have an advocate on the coaching staff and wasn't getting a chance to prove himself in practice.

Tom was always confident in his own abilities and

believed he was the top quarterback on the team. He thought if given the chance he'd be the right choice for the Wolverines. However, if he couldn't convince the coaching staff now that he was better than Dreisbach and Griese, when would he? Both would be back in 1997 and Dreisbach would likely also return in 1998. That meant maybe two more seasons of not playing. And by then who knows what recruit might come in to challenge Tom for the position? Could he afford to wait that long?

While both Griese and Dreisbach were talented, it's not like Michigan was having incredible success. It went 9–4 and 8–4 in Tom's first two seasons on campus, far below what Wolverine fans were accustomed to. There was intense pressure on Coach Carr to prove he deserved to be the head coach.

Tom began to think about leaving Michigan and transferring back home to Cal. He loved the University of Michigan, enjoyed Ann Arbor, and had made plenty of friends, including non-athletes he'd met in class and around campus. He enjoyed being around his teammates, especially when they weren't in the football facility. He and his friends formed an intramural basketball team. They hung out at one another's apartments. They competed in intense games of miniature golf. They were college kids, having a blast.

But he wanted to play football and didn't see a light at the end of the tunnel in Ann Arbor. He didn't think he'd ever climb the depth chart. He was impatient. Besides, Cal had hired Steve Mariucci as its coach before the 1996 season. Mariucci had a great reputation from his days as quarterbacks coach for the Green Bay Packers, where he'd worked with Brett Favre. Tom set up a meeting with Coach Carr.

"Coach," Tom said, "I think I am going to transfer."

"Why?" Coach Carr asked.

"I don't think I am getting a fair chance to play and I don't know if I'll ever play here," Tom said.

Coach Carr always carried himself like a gentleman. He was tough and demanding, but also approachable. He was like a favorite grandfather. He'd been coaching a long time, so he'd been through these kinds of conversations before and seen frustrated players such as Tom wrestle with this decision. Former coach Bo Schembechler had even coined a motto for the program, challenging men to keep fighting and believe: "Those who stay will be champions." It meant if you remained and worked, the success and glory would come. So Coach Carr didn't yell at Tom. He didn't snap at Tom. He didn't argue with Tom. He was direct with him. He told Tom if he wanted to transfer, then he would allow it, but he wanted Tom to hear his perspective before making a decision.

"It'll be the biggest mistake of your life, something you'll regret for the rest of your life," Coach Carr said. "You came here to be the best. You came here because of the great competition. If you walk away now, you'll always wish you had stayed and tried to compete, tried to become the best. If you leave, you'll always wonder what would have happened if you stayed."

He told Tom to think about it and come back the next day. If he still wanted to transfer, then Coach Carr would release him from his Michigan scholarship and wish him well.

Tom went back to his off-campus apartment and thought long and hard about what Carr had said. His father said he would support his decision but wanted Tom to make it with no regrets. Tom Sr. didn't believe transferring was the best option. He and his son had discussed many times how kids often just up and quit and run from challenges and problems rather than try to work through them. Tom Sr. was concerned his son wasn't getting a fair crack at Michigan, but in general, he believed sports should prepare someone for life, and in life you can't just transfer every time things don't go smoothly. If he left for Cal, he probably would play sooner, but would he then, like Coach Carr had said, forever regret not staying and trying to prove himself?

Tom returned to Coach Carr's office the next day with his decision.

"I'm staying," Tom said. "And I'm going to prove to you I am a great quarterback."

Coach Carr smiled. He was happy. Not just because he was keeping a young quarterback that he believed had potential to help the team, but also because he saw the old competitiveness that attracted Michigan to Tom Brady in the first place. At that moment, neither Carr nor Brady nor anyone else could have envisioned that Tom would become a future NFL star.

Carr did think Tom was someone who for the rest of his life would look back on that day and appreciate that when dealing with a tough situation, he'd stood his ground and worked to improve himself. Carr told Tom to stop worrying about what the other quarterbacks were doing and just focus on himself and improving every single day.

Stop trying to win the job and just do the job, he said to himself.

Tom's commitment to stay at Michigan reinvigorated him. It didn't mean things got any easier, though. The quarterback depth chart remained overloaded. Tom began working out at six a.m. each day in an effort to improve. He went to see a sports psychologist to work on his confidence. He watched more game tape to spot ways to get better and avoid repeating the same mistakes. He pushed himself to improve each day.

Yet just before the 1997 season began, Coach Carr announced Brian Griese would be the starter, Scott Dreisbach would be the backup, and Tom Brady would be the third-stringer. It's hard to believe today that a future NFL great, perhaps the best quarterback of all time, who has racked up Super Bowl and MVP trophies, couldn't even land the backup job on his college team!

Tom was frustrated. He felt he had beaten out Griese in training camp. But the only opinion that mattered was Coach Carr's. It turned out the coach made a wise decision.

Griese was a player who, like Tom, had been forced to fight his way to the top. Now with the job in hand in his final season, he made the most of it. He led Michigan to victories over the University of Colorado, Baylor University, and the University of Notre Dame to start the season, then rolled through the Big Ten. The Wolverines were loaded with talent, especially on the defense, where future NFL star Charles Woodson was the leader. Griese was a solid, mostly mistake-free quarterback who threw for 2,293 yards and seventeen touchdowns. Most importantly, the Wolverines went 11–0 in the regular season, went to the Rose Bowl as the number one team in America, and beat Washington State University. After the game they were named national champions.

Dreisbach was injured for much of the season, so Tom was the backup quarterback. He got into the action in just four games, completing twelve of fifteen passes. He wanted to play more, but once Griese started winning, there was no way Coach Carr was going to pull him out. The excitement of capturing a national title was more than enough to keep Tom patient. It was a magical time in Ann Arbor, the buzz of the fans growing each week.

Tom wanted to be a part of big-time college football and this was it, even if he was just the backup.

Griese graduated after that year and headed off to the NFL. Dreisbach continued to battle injuries. Heading into the 1998 season, Tom thought the path had finally cleared for him to become the starting quarterback at Michigan. He still had two years to play. He believed he was ready. His teammates believed in him. This is why he had stayed at Michigan, to get better while having the patience to outlast the tough times. The fact he won a national title in the process was a bonus. Now, finally, he was going to be the star.

Or so he thought.

"We all have experiences we look forward to," Tom said. "And when we get them, they don't always go the way we dreamed it."

6

Michigan

IN 1997, WHILE MICHIGAN WAS winning the national championship and Tom Brady was waiting his turn to become the starter in Ann Arbor, a few miles north a kid by the name of Drew Henson was tearing up the ball fields of Brighton High School. Many considered Henson the best high school athlete in America at the time. He threw for fifty-two touchdowns as a quarterback. He averaged twenty-two points a game on the basketball court. He walloped seventy homers at the plate, while clocking ninety-three miles per hour on his fastball. *Sports Illustrated* did a lengthy feature on him while he was still in high school, dubbing him "Golden Boy."

Everyone wanted Drew Henson. Not just every college program, every Major League Baseball franchise, too. Henson though, like Tom Brady, said he wanted to play college football, not baseball. The New York Yankees didn't care. They thought he was so talented they drafted him in the third round and offered him two million dollars to be a part-time minor-league prospect. This was almost unheard of, but they were certain they had found their third baseman of the future. The Yankees said Henson could play football in the fall, but once school let out for the summer, he had to come play in the minor leagues for them. Henson agreed. After all, that sounded like one great summer job.

Meanwhile, basically every major college football program in the country wanted Henson to come play for them. He nearly went to Florida State University. In the end, the pull of nearby Michigan was too much. Coach Carr landed the most coveted recruit in America.

Henson, unlike most Michigan quarterbacks, was not going to redshirt for a season. He was deemed ready from day one, perhaps because if he didn't play, Michigan knew he could leave and pursue a very profitable baseball career full-time with the Yankees. Henson had the kind of leverage over the program that Tom could never imagine. In addition, Henson arrived with great fanfare. The local media seemingly covered his every move, and fans who had watched or at least heard about this incredible quarterback for years wanted to know if he was for real and just how many games he'd win for Michigan. They wanted to see him play.

Adding to the excitement, Coach Carr declared before the season even began that Henson "without question is the most talented quarterback that I've been around." And Tom Brady? To the fans, he was just some backup who had barely ever played. They hardly knew his name.

Yet Coach Carr believed in competition. By the time the season began, he decided that despite the hoopla, Tom had won the starting job. "Tom Brady has paid his dues," Coach Carr explained that day to confused fans who wanted Henson. "He's worked extremely hard." At the same time, he said Henson had made quick progress and predicted he would play as a freshman.

Tom was just happy for the opportunity. He would finally get his chance. Sticking around had paid off. "I think everyone who is at Michigan is there for a reason," he said. "Everyone is talented. When you decide to come to a school like Michigan, you realize that there are great players here, and you realize that if you want to be the best, you've got to beat out the best."

Besides, as much as he was fighting Henson for the starting job, he liked the guy. They had become fast friends. Tom also believed in the importance of being a team player. "I don't think you go out and root against people," he said. "I think you go out and you perform as best you can and hope that it is better than the rest."

The season opener was at historic Notre Dame. It did not go as Tom Brady planned.

Coming off of a national title and playing in front of a *huge* crowd of eighty thousand fans in South Bend, Indiana, the Wolverines lost 26–20. The beginning of the Tom Brady era at Michigan was marked by disappointment. Tom actually played well, completing twenty-three of thirty-six passes for 267 yards. He also scored on a one-yard run. It wasn't a bad effort, but it wasn't enough to get the job done.

"Tom played with poise, toughness, and smarts," Coach Carr said.

However, a number of drives stalled out on field goals and the team was done in by poor tackling, fumbles, and a blocked field goal. "I felt comfortable," Tom said. "It is just a shame that we played our hearts out there today and we still lost. A loss like this just tears our hearts out."

As if a loss wasn't bad enough for Tom, late in the game with Notre Dame leading 36–13, Coach Carr put Henson in. The freshman responded by going five of eight and throwing a touchdown pass, exciting fans back in Michigan who still considered him the best option at quarterback.

If Notre Dame was a disappointment, the home opener against Syracuse University was a disaster. Syracuse jumped out to a 24–0 lead and later led 38–7. Tom didn't play well. He threw an early interception and completed just thirteen passes. The defense struggled. The offense failed to move the ball. Nothing went right. Trailing 17–0, Coach Carr sent Drew Henson in to replace Tom. The vision of Henson taking the field produced a huge roar from the frustrated crowd at Michigan Stadium.

On the bench, the cheering hurt Tom. In the stands, it crushed his family. They knew how hard he had worked to get to this point, how much he had given the school. They began to question whether Tom was again being treated unfairly. Tom, however, was long past that stuff. He had made a decision to stick with Michigan, no matter what. Nothing was going to stop him now, not even an 0–2 start, a benching, and fans cheering against him.

"If you're mentally strong enough, coming in and out of games is not a problem," Tom said at the time. "I'll bounce back. I've got a lot of pride at stake. Don't worry about me, I'll be back."

That was the kind of fight Coach Carr was looking for—a player who wasn't blaming coaches or teammates for the Wolverines' struggles, but putting everything on his own shoulders.

Carr stuck with Tom that season and soon the benching stopped. Michigan rattled off eight consecutive victories, including a 27–0 domination of then number nine ranked Penn State University, and a 27–10 victory over number eight University of Wisconsin. The Wolverines lost to archrival Ohio State University, but Tom threw for 375 yards in the face of relentless defensive pressure, again convincing his teammates that he was tough and not just some California pretty boy. Michigan finished out the season with victories over the University of Hawaii and the University of Arkansas in a bowl game. The Wolverines went 10–3 and won a share of the Big Ten title.

Tom completed 61.9 percent of his passes and tossed fourteen touchdowns. He wasn't the best college quarterback in America, but he won games. After the initial excitement, Henson was a traditional backup, throwing just forty-five passes during the season. Coach Carr made Tom earn his playing time—nothing was given—but once he got the starting job and settled in, he didn't come out.

"I don't think he played a bad game all season," Carr said.

Which is what made the start of the 1999 season so bizarre. Henson wasn't around for spring practice or summer conditioning because he was playing minor-league baseball for the Yankees. Tom was there the whole time, trying to prepare as much as possible for his final season at Michigan. Yet when training camp began in August, Coach Carr wouldn't commit to Tom being the starter, saying he would name the first-stringer at the kickoff of the opener against Notre Dame.

Publicly, Tom just shrugged it off. "I think it's

good to be pushed. It forces you to stay sharp and perform well."

That attitude is why the Michigan players voted to name Tom a team captain for the season. Four years prior, he'd come to Ann Arbor as an unknown recruit from the West Coast, a seventh-string quarterback who'd had to redshirt his first season. He'd still been uncertain if he could even play at this level. Now he was one of the three team captains, a prestigious honor at a prestigious football program.

Years later, Tom would return to Ann Arbor and speak to the 2013 Michigan team. By this point he was a superstar, an MVP, and a Super Bowl champion. He still saw himself as a Michigan Man, though.

"Now, I didn't have an easy experience," Tom told the Michigan players. "I didn't come in as a top-rated recruit. I didn't come in with every opportunity to play right away. I had to earn it. And you know the greatest honor I've ever received? I was named team captain. That, to this day, is the single greatest achievement I've ever had as a football player, because the men in this room chose me to lead the team."

In his senior year, Tom's leadership was being tested as the media kept asking about the quarterback competition and tried to see if he and Drew Henson were rivals. "Drew and I have a very good relationship," Tom said. "He respects what I do and I respect what he does. I enjoy Drew very much. He is very intelligent and has a great sense of humor."

Michigan beat Notre Dame in the opener, 26–22, with Tom leading a late-game touchdown drive to seize the victory. Tom went seventeen for twenty-four on the day for 197 yards. The thing that had fans talking, though, was Coach Carr's unorthodox and unexpected decision at quarterback that season. He decided that Tom would play the first quarter of games, Henson would play the second quarter, and then at halftime the coaches would decide who looked better and let that person play in the second half. No one had ever heard of such a system before. Fans and media wondered how any quarterback could relax and play well knowing they could get pulled from the game so quickly.

"I like them both," Coach Carr said. "If they continue to play well, I have no problem continuing to play both of them."

Back in San Mateo, Tom Sr. and the family didn't take the news well. They thought it was another attempt to undermine Tom's confidence. They couldn't understand why Coach Carr was treating him that way. Still, they never complained. In the five seasons Tom was at Michigan, his parents never called or met privately with Coach Carr to discuss their son or the team. They felt it was important to stay back. Carr was Tom's coach, not their coach. And once Tom had decided to stick with Michigan, he had to live with whatever came his way.

Privately, neither quarterback liked the system either. Neither one knew what was going to happen each week. Tom was certain he was the better player. Publicly and to their teammates, however, they behaved with integrity and said it was a good idea that would help the club. Tom wanted to display leadership and *this*, biting his tongue and putting on a smile for the sake of his teammates, was leadership. At Michigan, Bo Schembechler's most famous speech talked about the importance of "the Team, the Team, the Team." That was the culture of the program. Tom Brady wanted to exemplify that. He put a positive spin on everything.

It paid off. In the first five games, Tom earned the second-half start four times. Michigan started 5–0.

Then came the sixth game, at Michigan State University. Coach Carr gave Henson the nod for the second half this time, but he struggled and Michigan fell way behind, 27–10. Tom was reinserted and led a big comeback that just fell short, 34–31. Tom was thirty of forty-one on passing attempts for 285 yards and two touchdowns. Coach Carr had seen enough. He named Tom Brady the full-time starter and ended the platoon system. "Tom separated himself," Carr said. Finally, at last, Tom didn't have to look over his shoulder.

"I've always respected and admired Tom," Carr said. "Not just as a quarterback but as a leader. I assure you he did not want to share the quarterback job and yet as the head coach it's my decision to look at the big picture. There aren't many guys I have coached that could handle the situation like Tom did, and that is one of the reasons I felt comfortable in doing it because I knew what kind of a guy he is. You need a special guy at quarterback. In the long term, I think Tom will be able to say it was the most difficult situation he has been in. And he handled it extremely well. He gained in the eyes of his teammates and stature because he put his team first."

Brady agreed. No, he wasn't always happy sharing the job, but the stress Carr put him under prepared him for nearly anything.

Once he was the full-time starter, his play improved. Michigan lost to Illinois in a shootout and then never lost again. That included Tom leading two late touchdown drives to win at Penn State and a 24–17 victory over rival Ohio State in his final game at Michigan Stadium. His Wolverine career ended in the Orange Bowl, with Michigan defeating Alabama in a thrilling 35–34 overtime classic. Tom was thirty-four of forty-six for 369 yards and four touchdowns, twice leading Michigan back from fourteen-point deficits. The Wolverines finished the year ranked fifth in the nation.

It had been a long and twisting journey in Ann Arbor for Tom. Success came slow. He thought about leaving, but decided to stay. He made incredible friends, on and off the team. He won the respect of his coaches. He prepared for life by earning a degree with an emphasis in business and psychology, leaving with a 3.3 grade point average. He interned at the investment firm Merrill Lynch, just in case football didn't work out. His team earned a national championship and two Big Ten Championships.

And most of all, he learned to keep pushing, keep battling, keep trying to improve, all while being a loyal teammate.

Coach Carr once told him leaving would be the biggest mistake of his life. What Carr didn't say, but was equally as true, is that staying was therefore the best decision of his life.

"I wouldn't change it for anything in the world," Tom said.

He would need everything he learned in high school and college, and then some, in the National Football League.

7

The NFL Draft

IN HIS FINAL YEAR AT MICHIGAN, Tom Brady completed 62.8 percent of his passes for 2,586 yards. He tossed twenty touchdowns against six interceptions. His numbers were good but not great, in part because he had to share so much playing time with Drew Henson.

The best thing Tom had going for him was Michigan's 10–2 record his senior year. Plus there were his numerous comebacks, including the victories over powerhouses Penn State and the University of Alabama. He played, and delivered, against the toughest competition.

He also had Coach Carr touting him, "Tom is going to play in the NFL. He has every attribute you'd want." In the NFL, though, Carr's words didn't matter as much as his actions. Out of loyalty, college coaches always talk up their players. If Tom Brady was so good, why hadn't he been the full-time starter until the second half of the season? Why would Carr platoon him with Drew Henson?

"It was a red flag," New England Patriots Coach Bill Belichick said. "You don't normally have NFL quarterbacks share a starting job their senior year."

All Tom could do was try to convince them he was legit. He knew he wouldn't be a top pick or even a first- or second-rounder. He just wanted a chance.

The biggest event leading up to the draft is the annual NFL Combine in Indianapolis. The NFL invites three hundred to three hundred and fifty players, the ones who are likely draft picks, to come in for a few days to show off their abilities. They are weighed, measured, and then run through a series of skill tests—bench press, forty-yard dash, cone drill, even an intelligence test called the Wonderlic. Quarterbacks are also asked to make a series of passes. Hundreds of scouts, coaches, and general managers sit in the stands and watch. Dozens of cameras film everything, both for the NFL Network live broadcast and so teams can later watch a player and break down small, specific things such as a quarterback's footwork on a three-step drop.

There are no secrets after the Combine. You can't just say you can run the forty-yard dash in 4.4 seconds. You have to prove it. While it doesn't always predict success or failure, scouts pay close attention to everything that happens there.

Tom did not have a very good Combine. He was measured at six foot four and weighed in at 211 pounds, which was tall but thin. He wasn't all that muscular. His forty-time was 5.28 seconds, among the slowest ever recorded for a quarterback. His vertical leap was just 24.5 inches, also one of the lowest ever recorded. He was not an elite athlete.

There is far more to being a quarterback than just athletic ability, of course. You need someone who can "read" defenses and realize where and when a receiver might get open, then fire passes into tight areas and heavy coverage. That's more important than someone who can quickly run forty yards in a straight line. QBs almost never run forty yards at a time.

Still, Tom's numbers didn't compare to other

athletic or even average quarterbacks. Cam Newton, for example, is considered a very athletic quarterback. He's also a great quarterback, having led the Carolina Panthers to the Super Bowl and being named NFL MVP. He attended the Combine in 2011. He measured six foot five, 248 pounds, and ran a 4.65-second forty-yard dash with a thirty-five-inch vertical leap. He went number one overall in the draft that year. Tom was never going to be Cam Newton; even Tom admitted he was "slow, slow, slow."

Then during the throwing drills, Tom looked okay, but not great. His arm wasn't as strong as some of the other players'. His footwork wasn't as polished. No matter how much practice he went through, he was still limited. A football fan would point out that it is one thing to throw a ball under ideal circumstances, in a workout inside a domed stadium. It is another to do so in the fourth quarter, in the middle of a snowstorm when you are about to be sacked. That isn't how the Combine worked, though.

The NFL scouting report on Tom that came out of the Combine was harsh. It listed Tom's weaknesses as such: "poor build, skinny, lacks great physical stature and strength, lacks mobility and ability to avoid the rush, lacks a really strong arm, can't drive the ball downfield, does not throw a really tight spiral, system-type player who can get exposed if forced to ad lib, gets knocked down easily." Not everyone was totally down on Tom. ESPN's Mel Kiper called him a "smart, experienced, big-game signal caller," although he noted "he doesn't have the total package of skills."

Tom just didn't always look or move like an NFL quarterback. His greatest attributes remained his competitiveness, leadership, and ability to remain calm under pressure. You can't measure those on a stopwatch. There wasn't much Tom could do except hope that NFL teams saw how great he was on the field at Michigan, rather than how slow he was running cones in a Combine drill. It was frustrating. Once again, he was doubted.

Later that spring he attended a San Francisco 49ers camp held for local college prospects and guys who had grown up in the area. The coach of the 49ers by then was Steve Mariucci, the coach Tom had considered transferring to Cal–Berkeley to play under. It turns out Tom was lucky he didn't transfer from Michigan. Coach Mariucci returned to coaching in the NFL after just one season at Cal, so he would have been gone from Cal by the time Tom got there. Now Mariucci was getting an up-close view of Tom, who was hopeful he would turn the head of his old hometown coach.

It's not easy scouting quarterbacks. NFL teams make mistakes all the time and this day was one of them. Tom threw just eight or nine times before running another slow forty-yard dash. Mariucci wasn't overly impressed. Neither was San Francisco's general manager, Bill Walsh, who'd been the legendary coach when Joe Montana and Steve Young were the quarterbacks. Bill Walsh knew quarterbacks. He didn't see Tom as worth a high draft pick.

The 2000 NFL draft was held at Madison Square Garden in New York City. Many of the top prospects were invited to come and hear their name called. Tom was not one of those, so he watched with his family back in San Mateo. Rather than sit through the early rounds of the draft where he was unlikely to be selected, Tom and his father decided to go play golf to get their minds off of things. The entire day passed without Tom being picked. Three other quarterbacks were selected instead.

The New York Jets took Chad Pennington of

Marshall University with the eighteenth overall pick. That was a good choice; Pennington would become a starter despite dealing with shoulder issues. With the sixty-fifth pick overall, San Francisco took Giovanni Carmazzi out of Hofstra University, a small program in New York.

"That one hurt," Tom Sr. said. "We had been 49er season ticket holders all these years."

Carmazzi hadn't accomplished nearly as much as Tom in college, but he was bigger, stronger, and faster than Tom. That's what San Francisco liked. It was a risk, and it wouldn't pan out—Carmazzi wasn't good enough and never played a single regular season snap in the NFL. Finally, with the seventy-fifth pick, the Baltimore Ravens took Chris Redman, who had put up incredible numbers as a four-year starter at the University of Louisville. Redman went on to be a long-time backup in the league, about right for a third-round pick.

The Bradys were frustrated but remained hopeful. Day two of the draft would bring rounds 4–7 and they figured Tom would get picked then. Tom rose early to watch the draft and stay by the phone. Pick by pick kept clicking by, though, and no one chose Tom. Finally, in the fifth round, the first quarterback of the day was selected—the only problem was, it wasn't Tom's name that was called. With the 163rd overall pick, Pittsburgh grabbed quarterback Tee Martin, who had won a national title at the University of Tennessee. Five slots later, New Orleans took Marc Bulger of West Virginia University.

The Bradys couldn't understand. Chad Pennington was understandable. These other players were not sure things. Teams were just gambling on guys rather than choosing Tom. The long, agonizing wait continued. With the 183rd pick, Cleveland took Spergon Wynn of Southwest Texas State University, a small school. This was the ultimate blow. Wynn had completed just 47.8 percent of his passes for thirteen touchdowns against fourteen interceptions. He didn't even have good stats despite playing lesser competition.

That was enough for Tom. He told his parents he couldn't deal with the pressure and disappointment. He headed for the door to take a walk around the block. He grabbed a baseball bat and once outside began swinging it in the air to blow off steam. "With each name selected, it was getting worse and worse," Tom Sr. said. Tom just kept asking what was wrong. Didn't anyone watch him against Penn State and Ohio State and Alabama?

Maybe not. It was clear very few teams had researched his career. Thankfully for Tom and New England fans, the Patriots had come prepared.

In 2000, the New England Patriots hired Bill Belichick to run and coach the team. Belichick had spent five years coaching the Cleveland Browns, but was fired for not winning enough games. He vowed that if he ever got another chance, he would run an organization that prided itself on preparation. This was his first draft for the Pats, which is why New England was one of the few teams that did its homework on Brady, among many other players.

Bobby Grier, the Patriots player personnel director, was the only NFL executive who called Coach Carr and asked about Tom and the situation with Drew Henson. "I told him, 'You will never regret drafting Tom Brady,'" Carr said. Meanwhile, quarterbacks coach Dick Rehbein personally flew to Ann Arbor to watch Tom work out that spring. Belichick had watched lots of Tom's game tape and the team invited Tom in for an interview during the Combine. They all decided to judge the player on how he played, not on how he looked in drills, or the fact that Coach Carr hadn't played him all the time. Since Tom was pegged as being a backup, if anything, they saw his ability to come in and out of games on a moment's notice as a positive attribute.

Belichick and the Patriots had Tom ranked as about a third-round pick on their draft board. That didn't mean they were going to pick him in the third round, though. Belichick inherited a roster with a lot of holes in it . . . except at quarterback. The Patriots had Drew Bledsoe, a popular veteran Pro Bowler who led the Pats to the Super Bowl during the 1996 season. Just a month before the draft, New England signed him to a ten-year, $103 million contract. They also had two capable backups. Simply put, they were all set at QB.

Therefore, Belichick prioritized drafting players at other positions, where the team was weaker. The team would go 5–11 that season—they needed a lot of help. In the first five rounds of the draft, New England took two offensive linemen, a defensive lineman, a running back, a tight end, and a safety.

"We had a lot of rebuilding to do in 2000, 2001," Belichick said. "We had a few good players, but once you got past those guys, there was a lot of things that needed to be changed."

Yet as the draft went on, the Patriots couldn't believe that Tom Brady hadn't been selected by someone who might need quarterback help. New England began discussing whether they had overrated Tom. Maybe everyone else was right and they were wrong? But then again, they kept pointing to the Combine interview, which allows coaches and scouts to learn about a player's personality. What everyone recalled about Tom was that he was extremely confident. He carried himself like he was the best quarterback in the entire draft.

New England liked his story of rising from seventh string at Michigan to becoming team captain. They liked that he was a guy who might walk into camp and not be intimidated. No one on the Patriots' staff thought he would become the player he would. If they had, they would have selected Tom early in the draft and not risked losing him. They did think he was a far better prospect than anyone else they could get in the sixth round. So even though taking a quarterback made almost no sense, Belichick decided to draft Tom Brady with the 199th pick overall. They went with the best available player, even if they didn't need him.

By then, Tom had returned from his walk. The phone at his parents' house rang. He answered.

"Coach Belichick would like to speak to you," a voice said. And soon, there was Bill Belichick on the line.

"I was just so happy to be drafted at that point,"

Tom said. Yes, the depth chart was stacked, which meant there was no guarantee that Tom would even make the roster. He didn't care. He believed in himself. He knew he would find a way. "Once you are in the NFL, it doesn't matter if you are a first-round pick or a sixth-round pick," he said. "You have to deliver."

When he arrived in New England for his first training camp, he walked up to Patriots owner Robert Kraft and introduced himself.

"Hello, Mr. Kraft. I'm Tom Brady," Tom said.

Kraft laughed and shook his hand.

"I know who you are," Kraft said. "You're our sixth-round pick out of Michigan."

Tom nodded but wanted the owner to know that he wasn't just another late-round pick trying to make the team.

"I'm the best decision this organization has ever made," Tom said.

8

Rising Up

Iᴛ'ꜱ ʜᴀʀᴅ ᴛᴏ ɢᴇᴛ ᴀ ᴊᴏʙ as a professional football player. It's even harder to keep it. Someone is
always trying to beat you out. While fans focus on
the few stars who have long careers, many of their
teammates shuffle through season to season or
even week to week. The average length of a career
is about 3.3 seasons, which is why players often joke
that the NFL shouldn't stand for "National Football
League" but "Not For Long."

Tom knew that when he reported to Foxborough,

Massachusetts, for preseason camp in August of 2000. No player is guaranteed a roster spot, especially not a sixth-round pick coming into a position with three established veterans ahead of him.

But Tom immediately carried himself with the confidence he displayed to Robert Kraft. Competition was his specialty. He didn't know any other way of doing things other than taking each practice rep, each drill, each wind sprint like his career depended on it. It was the Michigan Way.

"If I didn't practice well during the week in college, I didn't know if I was going to start the game," Tom said. "So when I got to the NFL, I had the same mentality. Every practice I was fighting for my job."

Right away Coach Belichick realized the Patriots had made a wise selection in the sixth round. "He's a good, tough, competitive, smart quarterback," Belichick said at the time.

Tom's first ever NFL game was a preseason contest called the Hall of Fame Game. It is played annually in Canton, Ohio, the same weekend the Pro Football Hall of Fame enshrines its newest members. The entire weekend is festive and fun. That year, the Hall inducted two of Tom's favorite

49ers, quarterback Joe Montana and defensive back Ronnie Lott. The Patriots would also play against San Francisco, allowing Tom to show his hometown team what they missed.

He didn't play much, but he completed three of four passes late in the game. It was enough to impress Belichick. Across the way, Giovanni Carmazzi, whom the 49ers took in the second round, went just three of seven and was sacked twice. He looked overwhelmed. It would be a sign of what was to come. San Francisco fans still lament that their team chose him rather than Tom Brady.

By opening day, the Patriots made a move that surprised many around the NFL. They decided to keep Tom on the roster, carrying four quarterbacks, whereas most teams have three. Almost no one else could understand it. Drew Bledsoe would be the starter. Why not just have one extra quarterback and use those extra roster spots for more defensive help?

Belichick was undeterred. "Too many quarterbacks is a lot better of a situation than not enough," Belichick said. He saw a lot in Tom Brady. That didn't mean Tom would play as a rookie. He didn't. He spent the year learning from Bledsoe and Belichick. He got in a game just once, completing one pass late in a 34–9 loss to Detroit on Thanksgiving Day. The team went 5–11, the only losing season Belichick and Brady would have in New England (as of 2018).

By the 2001 camp, Tom established himself as Bledsoe's primary backup. The two quarterbacks ahead of him the previous year were released. Belichick now believed he had a good team in New England that could compete for the playoffs. He would carry just two QBs. Tom saw his opportunity coming. He became great friends with Drew Bledsoe, but he wanted to play, and believed he was better than even the star of the team. He knew from his days at Michigan that if he ever got out on the field, he needed to convince the coaches to never take him off it. And that meant being prepared when the opportunity came.

"You never want to see anyone else do your job," Tom said. "I just thought, 'Once I get my chance, I'm going to be ready.'"

His chance came in the second game of the season against the rival New York Jets. The game had been delayed a week due to the terrorist attacks of September 11, 2001. The pregame was emotional, with the playing of the national anthem and everyone saluting the flag. In the fourth quarter, with the Jets leading 10–3, Bledsoe tried to scramble for a first down. He was hit hard by Jets linebacker Mo Lewis, one of the biggest, toughest players in the NFL. Standing on the sideline, Tom said it was the loudest collision he'd ever heard in football. It was so violent Bledsoe's face mask broke, and after the game he was taken by ambulance to the hospital, where doctors had to stop internal bleeding.

Tom was soon in the game, with a chance to play in a critical moment. The Jets still led by seven with just 2:16 remaining. Tom drove the Patriots down the field but couldn't score a touchdown.

New York won. The NFL would never be the same.

It was apparent that Drew Bledsoe would be out for more than just a series or two, or even a game or two. He was seriously injured. Tom and everyone on the Patriots loved and respected Bledsoe, who had been the team leader for nearly a decade. They worried about his health. Yet they have a saying in the NFL, where injuries are common: "Next Man Up." In this case, that next man was twenty-four-year-old Tom Brady, finally given the opportunity he had long dreamed of getting. He was an NFL starter, and he knew no matter how good Bledsoe was that he would remain an NFL starter only as long as he played well and proved he was better than anyone else trying to take his job.

Tom's first start was a home game against the Indianapolis Colts, which had its own young quarterback in Peyton Manning. Peyton was the son of former NFL star Archie Manning, and the number one pick out of the University of Tennessee. Also, Peyton had a younger brother named Eli, who at that point was a star at the University of Mississippi but would soon become the quarterback for the New York Giants. No one could have predicted it at the time, but this was the first of many meetings to come between Tom Brady and one of the Manning brothers, a rivalry that would include multiple playoff games and legendary Super Bowls.

New England won 44–13. Tom was solid but not spectacular. The Patriots returned two Peyton Manning interceptions for touchdowns. Tom did show he belonged, though, and continued to get comfortable. His most memorable regular season game came in week five against the San Diego Chargers, with the Patriots trailing 26–16 in the fourth quarter. Down by a decent margin, New

England's chances of winning were looking pretty weak. But Tom had proven at Michigan that he wasn't the type to get intimidated. He led two late scoring drives to tie San Diego before winning the game in overtime. Tom showed the league his ability to come from behind—it was a sign of things to come.

By the end of the season, the Pats had reeled off six consecutive victories to win the AFC East division with a record of 11–5, earning a trip to the postseason. Bledsoe had returned from injury on November 13, but Brady, as he thought would be the case, kept the starting job. Belichick wasn't going to mess with success.

Tom completed 63.9 percent of his passes that year, for 2,843 yards. He threw eighteen touchdowns and twelve interceptions. His teammates had grown to appreciate his poise under pressure. By the end of a season that had started with Tom not knowing if he would even play much, he was named to the Pro Bowl and on his way to the playoffs.

Tom Brady's first playoff game was in Foxborough. The Patriots once played in the city of Boston and were known as the Boston Patriots. In 1971, they moved to a new stadium in the small town of Foxborough, south of the city. They decided to rename themselves the New England Patriots. While the team plays in Massachusetts, they have fans from the other small states of the Northeast—Connecticut, Maine, New Hampshire, Rhode Island, and Vermont. That region is called New England. Foxborough actually sits less than ten miles from the Rhode Island border and visiting teams often stay in that state's capital, Providence, rather than in Boston, the night before a game.

The Patriots were set to play the Oakland Raiders on the evening of January 19, 2002, when a snowstorm swept through the area. The field was soon covered. The grounds crew used small plows to clear the yard lines and sidelines. The flakes cascading down through the air made the stadium look like it was inside a snow globe. Just getting to the stadium was tough, with slippery roads causing traffic to back up. Tom thought he had given himself plenty of time to make it, but when he was stuck in traffic two and a half hours before the game, he had to call the Patriots head of security and tell him he wasn't sure if he, the starting quarterback, would arrive in time. The Patriots called the local police, who went and found where Brady was stuck, turned on their sirens to clear traffic, and gave him an escort to the stadium. Tom made it in time for warm-ups.

It was that kind of night, but Tom was right at home. His decision to play college football in Michigan paid off. He was comfortable playing and practicing in the cold, snow, sleet, and ice. "Michigan weather," he called it. He may have been from California, just across the Bay from where the Oakland Raiders played, but by now he craved the harsh conditions of the Midwest or Northeast. In an effort to show the Raiders that the cold wouldn't bother him, Tom took the field for pregame warm-ups wearing just a T-shirt. He smiled and pretended he was warm.

Traditionally, NFL teams concentrate on running the ball in this kind of weather. It's safer than risking the ball slipping out of their quarterback's hands as he tries to pass, or having throws wobble in the air and get intercepted. Tom's comfort in the weather, however, allowed Bill Belichick's team to pass the ball. Tom threw fifty-two times that night, completing thirty-two for 312 yards.

The game is famous for a few memorable plays. The first came in the fourth quarter, with Oakland leading 13–3 and Tom driving the Patriots toward a touchdown. Tom dropped back to pass but was sacked by his former Michigan teammate Charles Woodson. The ball came free and the Raiders recovered, which spelled doom for the Pats, who were running out of chances—and time.

However, after reviewing the play, the referees later ruled New England kept possession because of the little known "tuck rule." Though Tom was trying to tuck the ball away, because his arm was still moving forward when it was knocked out of his hand, the play was deemed an incomplete pass, not a fumble. For weeks and even years following the play, fans and analysts argued over whether or not the controversial decision was the right one. To this day, Raiders fans and players complain about the call.

Whether the tuck rule was a good rule wasn't Tom's problem. He took advantage of the reversal and soon scrambled into the end zone on a six-yard run. The field was so slippery that when he tried to spike the ball in celebration, he lost his footing and fell down. All he could do was laugh. It was now 13–10 with 7:52 remaining.

Tom wound up leading another scoring drive that ended when kicker Adam Vinatieri blasted a remarkable line drive forty-five-yard field goal through the snow and wind. The Pats won it in overtime on another Vinatieri field goal, booted through after his teammates got on their hands and knees and cleared inches of snow from where he was going to kick it, providing him firm footing. Patriots fans responded by throwing snow in the air. The players celebrated by making snow angels.

The Pats were huge underdogs the following week at Pittsburgh. New England had other plans, winning 24–17 to advance to the Super Bowl. Tom was injured during the game. He was replaced by none other than Drew Bledsoe. It was a reversal from early in the season. Bledsoe was ready and played well, even throwing a critical touchdown pass. That's how the Patriots were, though, a true team.

In the Super Bowl, the Saint Louis Rams presented New England's toughest challenge. They had won the championship the season before and their high-powered offense was known as "The Greatest Show on Turf." They had gone 14–2 and averaged over thirty-one points a game. The Rams quarterback Kurt Warner was named the league MVP and running back Marshall Faulk was the Offensive Player of the Year. They had two star wide receivers in Isaac Bruce and Torry Holt. New England was still an upstart team, with Bill Belichick in just his second season and Tom Brady new on the scene. Since Tom was healthy enough to play in the Super Bowl, he remained the starter and Bledsoe the backup. Still, most people predicted the Rams would win by two touchdowns and cruise to a championship. This was a team with dynasty potential. The game was David vs. Goliath.

The Patriots loved being overlooked. Tom was as confident as ever. In the locker room before the game, his teammates wondered if he would be nervous until they caught him leaned up against a wall, dozing off for a nap. The Patriots liked being known as a team that didn't need any big-name star players to be successful, so they came up with a novel idea to emphasize that. TV networks like to introduce players individually before the Super Bowl, having each guy run out of the tunnel one at a time. The announcers talk about the stars to the large TV audience, many of whom only watch one game a year. New England said they wouldn't do it that way. They wanted to be introduced as a team and have everyone run out on the field at the same time.

"We play together," cornerback Ty Law said. "We're a team."

Then they went out and proved it.

The defense slowed the Rams offense down. Ty Law intercepted Warner and returned it for a touchdown. Brady threw a touchdown pass. Vinatieri kicked a field goal. New England led 17–3 at halftime. Fans across the country were stunned. The question was, could the Patriots seal the deal?

In the second half, the Rams, as all great teams do, began coming back and eventually tied the game at seventeen. The Pats got the ball with 1:21 remaining on their own seventeen-yard line. On television, the announcers predicted they'd take a knee, run out the clock, and go to overtime rather than risk a mistake that deep in their own territory. An interception or fumble could cost them the game. With a young quarterback, that was risky.

Belichick and Brady saw it differently and instead went out and tried to win. Tom quickly moved them down the field, completing five passes until they reached the Rams' thirty-yard line. To stop the game clock from winding down to zero, Tom quickly spiked the ball with just seven seconds remaining. Adam Vinatieri calmly ran out on the field. As time expired he kicked a forty-seven-yard game winner to give New England a shocking upset and its first

Super Bowl title ever! Since it wasn't snowing inside the New Orleans Superdome, the kick was practically easy for Vinatieri.

That final scoring drive and victory made Tom Brady a legend.

Tom was named the Super Bowl MVP. He hadn't even been the starter when the season began. Part of his job as MVP was to film a commercial for the Walt Disney Company, which included saying the famous phrase "I'm going to Disney World," which has been a tradition in postgame interviews at the Super Bowl for years. Then the next day Tom was expected to fly to Orlando, Florida, and serve as the grand marshal in the daily Walt Disney World parade. There was one problem—team rules said he was supposed to fly home to Boston on the team plane.

Hours after winning the Super Bowl, Tom went to Belichick's room at the team hotel and asked if he could skip the team flight and go to Disney World. Belichick just laughed.

"Of course you can," Belichick said, according to *Sports Illustrated*. "How many times are you going to win the Super Bowl?"

Tom was determined to find out.

9

Dynasty

Tom Brady was now a superstar. He was a household name. He was famous.

The dramatic Super Bowl victory and his story of overcoming doubters made him extremely popular, not just in New England, but around the country. Companies began seeking him out to endorse their products. TV shows asked him to guest star. He even was a judge at the Miss USA Pageant. He used to be able to eat dinner out at a restaurant and either go unnoticed or have other customers not care that a reserve player was there. Now he was swarmed for autographs. An estimated eighty-seven million people watched the Super Bowl and now everyone wanted to know everything about him. Who was his family? What did he do for fun? Did he have a girlfriend?

That fifty-three-yard championship-winning drive against the Rams changed everything in his life.

His job was to make sure the changes were good ones. For example, rather than golfing with his dad at just their local course, they might now play at Augusta National Golf Club, the home of The Masters. Meanwhile, he needed to avoid the bad changes, such as having all the attention, accepting party invitations, and allowing celebrity interactions distract him from actually playing football.

Tom was just twenty-four at the time and while he had become the youngest starting quarterback to ever win a Super Bowl, that didn't guarantee he'd win another or even have a long career in the NFL. It's not uncommon for players to have a big season or two and then flame out. For the 2001 season, Tom was paid $387,000, which is a great deal of money by almost any standard other than an NFL star quarterback. That was a backup's salary. While he would soon sign a lucrative long-term deal with New England that would make him very wealthy, at that point in the off-season after the Super Bowl, he was not some millionaire living in a mansion who would never have to worry about money again. He needed to keep his job.

So while the attention was fun, he also feared it.

"I understand what it takes to win in the NFL," Tom said. "And it's not just a daily commitment; it's a life commitment. Every decision you make is a conscious decision to try to help your team win, whether that's in March or that's in September or whether that's in November. You can't just flip the switch when it matters. The competition is always on. It never goes away. You're either getting better or you're getting worse."

That meant a summer of six a.m. workouts. That meant eating nutritious meals. That meant getting to bed early to give his body proper time to rest. Where some may have thought Tom Brady would become a Hollywood celebrity after winning the Super Bowl, the reality was the opposite. Winning one just made him want to win again. He was still as hungry and humble as that high school kid stumbling through the five-dot drill on his parents' backyard patio. Scoring touchdowns on national television is fun. The discipline that goes into it all year around is not, unless you embrace that and find joy in the work.

Tom had a partner in this journey, his coach Bill Belichick. Fans know Belichick for his gruff demeanor, his habit of wearing a ratty, hooded sweatshirt on the sidelines, and his frequent clashes with the media. Belichick has coached in the NFL since 1975 and his old-school style is based on fundamentals. Get the small things right and the big things will take care of themselves. He is very demanding of his players, yet he works even longer hours than they do trying to build and coach the team. It's how New England chose Brady. For some players, New England is not an enjoyable place to play because of Belichick. For others, having a coach that matches your competitiveness and commitment is ideal. Belichick has even been able to bring out the highest potential in players who acted up or argued with a coach on a different team. If nothing else, everyone respects him.

"He's very consistent as a coach," Tom said. "I think he expects and demands that we're always at our best. I'd say that he coaches me the same way that he coached me the day that I got here. The goal is really greater than the individual. On our team, it's interesting, there really is no separate treatment for different players. The rookies are expected to perform and act the same as the veteran guys. It's great as a player on our team, because you really don't have to hold the other players accountable because the head coach does it."

Beyond his exacting standards, something else Belichick is famous for is cutting or trading a player if he thinks it will help his team get better. He loves his players, but the moment he sees an opportunity to improve his team, he'll take it. Which is why, before the 2002 season, Belichick traded Drew Bledsoe to Buffalo in exchange for a first-round draft pick. Tom was going to be the starter, so the team didn't need Drew any longer. Bledsoe had been the franchise quarterback until Tom Brady beat him out. Then he was trade bait.

Belichick's aggressive strategy doesn't just keep the roster churning and the talent sharp, it puts every player on notice. If he can dump a star player, he'll dump anyone. You better prove your worth if you want to stick around and win a championship.

Going in to the 2002 season, expectations were

high following a Super Bowl victory. Tom and the Patriots were no longer underdogs—they were the reigning champs. But it proved to be a come-back-to-reality year for Tom and his teammates, as they finished 9–7 and missed the playoffs.

Unfazed by their mediocre performance the year before, New England roared through the 2003 season. They racked up twelve consecutive victories to end the regular season, with Tom playing some of his best football yet. He threw for 3,620 yards and twenty-three touchdowns and enjoyed playing on a team with a ferocious defense. In the AFC Championship Game, the Patriots matched up against Peyton Manning and the Colts, the first truly high-profile matchup between the two star quarterbacks. In this one, Tom merely needed to be good, not necessarily great. He threw one TD and watched as the Pats defense picked off Manning four times (three of them by Ty Law) to snuff out the high-scoring Colts 24–14.

Making their second Super Bowl appearance in three seasons, Tom and the Patriots felt different this time around. They knew what to expect when they landed in Houston for the game, from the crowds to the media attention. They were playing the

Carolina Panthers and the game was a shootout, with thirty-seven points scored between the two teams in the fourth quarter alone. Tom set the Super Bowl record at the time for completions at thirty-two. He finished with 354 yards and three touchdowns. He even found himself in a familiar position. With the game tied at twenty-nine, he took over the Patriots offense with 1:08 left in the game. He completed four passes, drove New England to the Carolina twenty-three-yard line, and then watched as Adam Vinatieri drilled another Super Bowl–winning field goal. It was the same old story. Tom was again named Super Bowl MVP. His place as an elite quarterback in the league was now firmly secured.

That year the Super Bowl MVP won a free Cadillac. It was a sweet car, but Tom wanted it to go to better use than just getting driven around by him. After the first Super Bowl, he signed two hundred footballs, which Serra High School used as a fundraiser. This time he decided to donate the Cadillac to help raise money and show his appreciation for where he came from and where his career started.

"Everything I needed to know I began learning in those hallways," Tom said.

Serra set up a raffle. For twenty-five dollars you could buy a chance to win Tom Brady's Super Bowl Cadillac. You could buy as many chances as you wanted. Not only was the opportunity to win a new car for just twenty-five dollars incredible, winning Brady's Super Bowl Cadillac added to the excitement. The only mistake Serra made was underestimating the demand. It couldn't handle all the phone calls that poured in. By the time the drawing was held, $375,000 had been raised for school renovations. Sometimes it's nice to have a Super Bowl champion as an alumnus.

As good as the 2003 Patriots were, the 2004 Patriots may have been even better. Certainly the offense was, jumping from twelfth best in the league the year prior to fourth best. The defense remained as stubborn as ever. Tom threw for twenty-eight touchdowns and the team rode big running back Corey Dillon for twelve more TDs on the ground. New England started 6–0, which meant counting the final twelve straight wins at the end of the 2003 regular season and three victories in the postseason, it had won a record twenty-one consecutive NFL games. Pittsburgh stopped the streak, but New England steamrolled to another 14–2 record and the AFC East Division Title.

The playoffs brought another game against Peyton Manning and Indianapolis, and another opportunity for the Pats' defense to rise up— Manning threw another interception and didn't manage to throw for a touchdown. Leaning on a strong performance from Dillon and a dependable one from Brady, New England won 20–3. But the true test was still to come: Next up were the fearsome Steelers.

Pittsburgh went 15–1 that season, including beating New England, so it got to host the AFC Championship Game. The Steelers had the best defense in the league and the Patriots' major concern was that Tom had the flu and a 103-degree temperature the night before the game. He looked lousy huddling under blankets at the team hotel. He looked good on the field, though, throwing two touchdowns as the Pats blew up the scoreboard, jumping out to a 24–3 lead at the half before cruising to a 41–27 victory.

The Super Bowl was getting to be old hat now for the Pats, three appearances in four years. This one was against the Philadelphia Eagles in Jacksonville, Florida.

"It doesn't get old," Tom said. "The Super Bowl never gets old. There is one goal and that is to win the last game of the season. You can't do that unless you are here."

Complacency was not going to be a factor. Philadelphia was good, but New England was better, leading by ten until a late Eagles touchdown set the final score at Patriots 24–21.

For a third time in four seasons, red, white, and blue confetti fell from the post–Super Bowl sky and Tom got to hoist the Vince Lombardi Trophy. The victory cemented the Patriots as a dynasty, ruling over the NFL for an extended period. Tom and his teammates had now won nine consecutive playoff games. They'd proven themselves as one of the great groups of all time, a true team that found different ways to win with different stars stepping up. Football had become everything Tom hoped and dreamed it could be, the thrill of hard work paying off in triumph. He loved that everyone worked together to build something great. He loved the camaraderie. He loved his coaches and teammates.

When Bill Belichick picked Tom Brady in the draft, Belichick was a second-chance coach trying to prove he knew what he was doing. Tom, meanwhile, was an unheralded prospect trying to prove he belonged. Together they found their mirror image.

"No one works harder or prepares harder than Tom Brady," Belichick said.

"He has high expectations for our team," Tom said of Coach Belichick. "He has high expectations in the spring camps and they travel all the way through the football season. He wants us to all be at our very best. It doesn't stop. He walks into a team meeting room every day and says, 'All .right guys, this is a big day,' and he means it. He just doesn't say it the Wednesday of the Super Bowl week. He says it on a Wednesday in April. He understands that it is all a part of the building process to get to this point. I think the pressure is always on with him."

The perfect marriage of coach and player now ruled the NFL.

10

Streak

THERE IS A REASON dynasties are rare in the NFL. Winning one Super Bowl is difficult. Maintaining that level of play for three or four or five years is nearly impossible. Players get old. Players get injured. Players leave via free agency, when salary cap restrictions make re-signing them unaffordable. Assistant coaches get hired by other teams. The pieces that came together to form an elite squad could fall apart quickly.

The most amazing thing about the Tom Brady/

Bill Belichick–era New England Patriots is their consistency and their ability to find success while reworking the roster. Since 2003, the Pats have won at least ten games for fifteen consecutive seasons. The only team to do it longer was the San Francisco 49er squads Tom grew up watching, which did it sixteen seasons in a row from 1983 to 1998. New England wins the AFC East division pretty much every year. They reach the playoffs pretty much every year. They are the one constant in the NFL. It isn't easy. It's the hallmark of their greatness.

The 2005 season began with New England looking to win a third consecutive Super Bowl and fourth in five years. Then all their running backs got injured—including Corey Dillon and another solid back, Kevin Faulk. Tom had to pass more often. He led the NFL with twenty-six touchdowns and 4,110 yards. That wasn't the ideal offense for the Pats, though, and in a sport as competitive as football, even little things can derail a team.

They finished 10–6. In the playoffs, the Pats defeated Jacksonville in the wild card round, moving Tom's postseason record to 10–0. The following week they traveled to Denver and reality set in as the Broncos won 27–13. It was a good season by any measurement, except of course by the standards of Brady and Belichick.

In 2006, the Patriots, who went 12–4, thought they could get back to winning the Super Bowl. The problem was so did Peyton Manning and the Indianapolis Colts.

After losing twice in the playoffs to the Pats, Indy had slowly built up their roster in an effort to get past New England. Peyton was now in his ninth season, and was considered the most talented and productive quarterback in the NFL, but he had yet to reach a Super Bowl, let alone win it. That was usually because New England was in the way. Due to how the NFL sets its schedule each year, the two teams began playing annually during the regular season. They became the most anticipated regular season games of the year, Brady vs. Manning producing huge TV ratings. In 2006, Indy won the midseason clash, which is why the Colts got to host the AFC Championship Game despite the fact that the teams had the same regular season record. Many experts thought these were the two best teams in football. Whoever won, they said, would go on to win the Super Bowl.

The rivalry between the two franchises had

become intense. They were both great teams with lots of star players. Much of the interest centered on the quarterbacks. Fans of Manning liked to point to his superior stats and high-powered arm. Fans of Tom cited his ability to win games, and noted that at that point he had three Super Bowl rings to Manning's zero. It seemed like if you were an NFL fan, not just of the Pats or Colts, you had to pick a side.

Peyton grew up in the South, boasted a polite, funny, aw-shucks personality, was the son of a former NFL star (his dad, Archie), and came into the league with sky-high expectations. Tom was from California, looked like a movie star, dressed in the latest fashions, and arrived in the league with no one believing in him. They were opposites. Yet they were similar. Both were rising talents with enormous potential and enormous expectations. When one did something spectacular, the other usually followed. It could be setting an on-field record. Or it could be something off the field. Tom, for instance, once hosted *Saturday Night Live*. Two years later, Peyton hosted *Saturday Night Live*. Brady and Manning. Manning and Brady. It was everywhere.

In this AFC Championship Game, it looked like New England would again get the upper hand.

The Pats led 21–6 at the half and Peyton was again struggling against Bill Belichick's defense. Yet the Colts rallied during a wild second half that saw eight different scoring drives between the two teams. Unfortunately for New England, the last one was a Colts touchdown with one minute remaining to give Indy the 38–34 victory. It was one of the most exciting playoff games ever. Two weeks later, Peyton Manning and Indianapolis defeated Chicago to win the Super Bowl.

It was a bitter pill for Tom and New England to swallow, coming so close to another championship only to fail to achieve what they'd set out to accomplish. The thing was, for all their on-field competition, Tom and Peyton liked each other, texted encouragements to one another in the weeks they weren't playing, and even had each other's families over during the off-season. They met at Tom's first NFL start in 2001. Tom was a little-known backup, filling in for an injured Drew Bledsoe. Peyton, two years older, was already an established starter and the famous former number one pick in the draft. Yet it was Peyton who walked up to Tom, extended a hand to shake, and introduced himself.

"Hey, Tom, I'm Peyton," Manning said.

Tom laughed to himself and shook Peyton's hand. Of course he knew who Peyton Manning was. From there a friendship of sorts developed. Tom even learned from Peyton. Throughout his career, when new players were signed to the team, Tom took time to walk up to them in the locker room, extend his hand, and introduce himself. "Hi, I'm Tom Brady, I play quarterback." The starstruck newcomers couldn't believe one of the best players of all time was introducing himself to *them*. That was the point. Tom wanted them to see him as a teammate, not some intimidating, unapproachable star. Tom and Peyton were heated competitors, each standing in the way of the other's ultimate goal. But they left the arguing to their fans. At the same time, Tom Sr. and Archie Manning exchanged texts each Monday, sharing their perspective as dads of NFL QBs.

"We've always had a good relationship," Tom said. "He's always been someone I've really looked up to and studied and admired. He's always set a really high bar for how to play."

"All I can really say is Tom plays quarterback the way it is supposed to be played," Peyton said. "He's a really good guy."

Tom liked having strong relationships with other NFL players. He was particularly appreciative of his teammates and the work they put in under Coach Belichick. Yet he respected everyone in the league. While players often shout at each other on the field, or take shots at one another on social media or through the press, most offer respect for what it takes to make it in the NFL. They share a brotherhood, and while brothers often fight, in the end, they have each other's backs.

As Tom racked up Super Bowl wins and grew in prominence, there were a lot of stories and discussion about how NFL teams had blown it by not drafting him, and how Coach Carr should have never made him share playing time with Drew Henson at Michigan. Tom has always acknowledged using those slights as motivation. He won't apologize for that. Going 199th overall sticks with him. So does recalling the look of helplessness on his parents' faces as team after team let him slip by in the draft. He didn't like the criticism of others, though. He preferred to succeed with grace.

He has always been loyal to Coach Carr, even crediting the challenges Carr put him through for making him the mentally tough player he became. If it had been easy, he probably wouldn't have been as good of a player. And he hated what was said about Drew Henson, who had long been a friend and a teammate, not a rival. When Tom graduated, Henson went on to have a great junior season as Michigan's starting quarterback. He later played briefly for the Yankees in the major leagues before returning to football and playing two seasons for the Dallas Cowboys and Detroit Lions. If he had concentrated on one sport rather than two, he likely would have had even more success.

Then there were the so-called Brady Six—the quarterbacks drafted ahead of Tom in the 2000 draft. It's fair to criticize the general managers who drafted those players, but not necessarily the players. They weren't responsible for where they got picked. Besides, most of them turned out about as good as they were projected. Pennington was a starter with the Jets. Marc Bulger had an excellent career, starting ninety-five games, which is more than is expected as a sixth-rounder. Redman was a good backup. Fellow sixth-round picks Tee Martin and Spergon Wynn didn't last, but that's what happens with late-draft picks. About the only real bust was Giovanni Carmazzi.

Tom believed there was a way to motivate your-self without tearing down others. It's part of what makes him one of the NFL's most respected and popular players. He was also maturing. In 2007, he and his longtime girlfriend, the actress Bridget Moynahan, had a son together, John Edward Thom-as, whom they called Jack. Suddenly Tom wasn't just living for himself. He was a father and he began seeing the world differently. His relationship with Bridget didn't work out, but they remain committed co-parents to Jack.

Later on, Tom attended a charity gala in New York City. That's where he saw and met Gisele Bündchen, a native of Brazil who worked as a super-model. They were soon a couple. They eventually married and have two children of their own, a son, Benjamin, born in 2009, and a daughter, Vivian, in 2012.

"Becoming a father changed my life dramati-cally," Tom said. "Your life becomes very focused around your kids. A lot of things have been cut out over the years. I still have a lot of great friends. I just don't get to spend a lot of time with them. Family is my priority."

The Bradys have an exciting life. Tom is an NFL

superstar. Gisele is even better known around the world and is such a sought-after model and product endorser that she actually makes more money than her husband. Yet for all the fame and fortune, they pride themselves on being regular people, two devout Catholics who grew up in more traditional homes. His kids offer a nice balance to life, something other than football to focus on. As much as his kids love wearing his jersey and cheering for the Pats, when they were really young Tom was reminded the wins and losses only mattered so much.

"I have a four-and-a-half-year-old who is much more interested in the *Millennium Falcon* and his Lego sets than football," Tom joked before one big game.

11

Chasing Perfection

HEADING INTO THE 2007 SEASON, Bill Belichick decided Tom Brady needed some new weapons. The Patriots lacked star receivers. That would soon change.

During the 2007 NFL draft, Belichick made two trades. He gave Miami two draft picks for Wes Welker, a quick, sure-handed wide receiver, who would serve as a short pass threat for Tom. Belichick then sent a fourth-round selection to Oakland for Randy Moss, a brilliantly fast and talented receiver considered one of the best to ever play the game. Moss stood at six foot four and was capable of catching passes with one hand. He recorded a 4.38-second forty-yard dash time at the NFL Combine, one of the fastest ever. He also had a reputation as a difficult player to have on a roster. The only reason Moss was available was because he had been arguing with coaches and teammates in Oakland and his production dropped off. Belichick thought getting Moss into the disciplined system of New England and under the leadership of Tom would revitalize his career.

The plan proved to be a historically spectacular success. Welker was the perfect fit for Tom's accuracy; he could run short routes and pick up five, seven, nine yards at a time. He caught 112 passes that season for 1,175 yards and eight touchdowns. The year before, the Patriots leading receiver was Reche Caldwell with just sixty-one catches.

Moss meanwhile gave Tom the deep threat he never previously had. The chance to join New England motivated Moss, who was taller, faster, and more talented than nearly anyone who ever played football. Moss was also a guy who wouldn't try hard on a bad team he didn't trust. Surrounded by positive personalities, he was all in.

"Randy's a competitor," Tom said at the time. "He loves to play football. I think he does want to fit in. Being a Patriot and being a part of this team, it's about being smart, being physical, and putting the team first. That's why it's fun to play here."

Getting an entire team to rise to the standards of Belichick and Brady is not easy, but it is essential to success. Every player says they are willing to do this, but it's often different in reality when a coach is pointing out your mistakes or demanding you do better than maybe you even believe possible. Belichick never hesitated to yell at Tom in front of the team if Tom made a mistake. The star QB got no special treatment. He was just another player. When Patriots teammates saw Tom willing to be coached harshly, then they too were willing to be coached that way.

Then there was Tom's legendary work ethic. He prided himself on being the first one to Gillette Stadium each day. He is often in bed by eight or eight thirty at night, so driving from his home to Foxborough at five thirty a.m. was no big deal. Other players would arrive in the weight room at early times, say five forty-five or just after six a.m., only to find Tom already lifting. He'd greet them with a playful "Good afternoon," like they were late or lazy. They got the message. The best player was also the best worker. Altogether, it created a team attitude deemed "the Patriot Way" by Belichick and Brady.

Moss saw this from afar. He saw the way the team played together. Every competitive player wanted to be a Patriot. That's why Moss couldn't believe his luck when his phone rang and a voice on the other side said it was Bill Belichick and he wanted to trade for Randy to come to Foxborough. Moss was out at a nightclub and couldn't hear well through the noise. He figured he was being tricked.

"I thought it was a friend playing with my phone," Moss told ESPN. "I actually cussed him out. When he kept saying it was Bill Belichick, I knew he was serious. I started being apologetic because I had cussed the man." Belichick forgave him. But he made it clear that Moss was expected to come ready to work. Moss immediately did and fit in. "This is the best coached team I've been on," Moss said early in the season. "I'm just enjoying the ride."

The Pats played at the Jets in the season opener. Tom Brady and Randy Moss put on a show. Randy caught nine passes for 183 yards. He had one touchdown on a fifty-one-yard bomb after he out-sprinted three Jets defensive backs. "He just ran away from the defense," Tom marveled. "He ran about as far as I can throw it. I didn't have much more." Welker caught nine passes and New England blew the Jets out 38–14. The NFL was put on notice.

What happened throughout the rest of the season was unlike anything the sport of football had ever seen. The Patriots were unstoppable. Tom was never better, finding open wide receivers all over the field. The NFL is designed to have competitive games and make sure no team is too good or too bad. The NFL draft gives the best picks to the worst teams. A cap on how much money a squad can pay in salaries prevents stars from all going to the same team. Usually games are close and everyone is beatable. The famous saying "any given Sunday" is about how any team, even the worst, can beat any other team, even the best, if they bring all they have. That saying didn't apply to the 2007 Pats. No one was on their level.

After the Jets, they beat San Diego 38–14 and then Buffalo 38–7. In consecutive weeks they scored forty-eight at Dallas and forty-nine at Miami. Then they came home and beat Washington 52–7.

Two weeks later they crushed Buffalo, 56–10. The Pats plowed through the regular season, becoming the first team in NFL history to go 16–0 (the 1972 Miami Dolphins went 14–0 when the season was shorter).

The numbers were staggering. New England's 589 points that season was the most a team had ever scored at the time. Its plus-315 point differential (an average of nearly twenty points a game) was also a record. So was New England's twelve games of scoring twenty or more points. Tom completed a stellar 68.9 percent of his passes for 4,806 yards. He threw a then-record fifty touchdowns. He was named the Most Valuable Player in the NFL for the first time. Randy Moss caught twenty-three touchdowns, also a record. Eight Patriots were named to the Pro Bowl, the most since the legendary 1985 Chicago Bears.

Prior to that season, New England had already been a popular team, not just in Boston or Providence, but around the country. They became can't-miss television that season, though, because football fans couldn't believe the fireworks they were creating. Just about every game brought at least one unforgettable Tom-to-Randy pass and catch, usually more than one.

The Patriots won their first two playoff games to reach the Super Bowl at 18–0, just one game from perfection. Waiting across the way were the New York Giants. New England had defeated the Giants in the final game of the regular season, but it had been a narrow victory, 38–35. It gave the Giants confidence that they could compete in the Super Bowl in Glendale, Arizona. The Giants starting quarterback was Eli Manning, Peyton's younger brother. Just when Tom thought he had escaped one Manning, there was another.

The Super Bowl was unlike any other game for the Pats during the season. The Giants had studied up on Tom and his offense and came prepared. New York had a great pass rush and slowed the Pats' offense. The Giants led 10–7 in the fourth quarter until Tom hit Randy for a six-yard touchdown with 2:42 remaining to take a 14–10 lead. It looked like Tom had done it again, delivering another late-game Super Bowl–winning drive.

Except then Eli Manning got the ball on his own seventeen-yard line, determined to spoil Tom's party, and led the Giants down the field. In one of the most memorable plays ever, Eli barely avoided a sack only to scramble out of the pocket and launch the ball thirty-two yards to a leaping wide receiver named David Tyree, who grabbed the ball and held it against his helmet as he crashed to the ground, somehow maintaining control. The incredible, game-saving catch was nicknamed the "Helmet Catch."

Eli capped off the drive with a TD with thirty-five seconds left. And just like that, the perfect season was over. For Patriots fans, it was a painful loss because this may have been the best team in NFL history, just seconds from a 19–0 season. Tom felt the same way.

"I remember waking up in Arizona the next morning after an hour of sleep thinking, 'That was a nightmare. That didn't happen,'" Tom said.

The bad mood continued in 2008, when Tom was hit in the season opener and tore the anterior and medial cruciate ligaments (ACL and MCL) in his left knee. Doctors said he needed surgery and a year of rehabilitation to get healthy, so he wouldn't play again that season. After nearly winning the Super Bowl and breaking all sorts of passing records, he was done in week one. It was a reminder that everything can be taken away at any time. New England went 11–5 without him—a testament to Belichick's coaching and ability to find talent—but failed to make the playoffs.

Tom returned to health and to form in 2009. He threw twenty-eight touchdown passes and New England had moments of their old dominance. They beat Tennessee 59–0 in one game, scoring a record five touchdowns in a single quarter. They finished the season 10–6, though, and lost to Baltimore in the playoffs. The next year Tom was brilliant statistically, throwing for 3,900 yards and thirty-six touchdowns with just four interceptions. He won his second league MVP award. Yet the Jets upset the Pats in the opening round of playoffs.

Randy Moss had left the team by the 2011 season, but Belichick changed the offense to focus on two young tight ends, Rob Gronkowski (or "Gronk") and Aaron Hernandez. Both were fast and physical. Opponents struggled to cover them both at the same time. Welker meanwhile kept catching one hundred-plus passes as New England went 13–3. This was their best team since the near-perfect 2007 season, but when they got to the Super Bowl, there were Eli Manning and the Giants. Again.

The Super Bowl was played in Indianapolis that year. In preparation, teams come a week early and are assigned a practice facility. Usually one team gets the host NFL team's stadium and the other works out at a local college or even a big high school. The

Pats were given the Colts' building, with Tom suddenly getting dressed and practicing in the same locker room his rival Peyton Manning used. Tom joked that he was happy the Colts great pass rusher Dwight Freeney, who had sacked him many times, wasn't there to tackle him.

The game meant everything to Tom. He was now thirty-four years old in a sport where careers are generally short. For all the great success early in his career, it had now been seven seasons since he'd won a Super Bowl. He'd missed a year due to injury and been knocked out of the playoffs in the first round twice. He knew these opportunities weren't guaranteed.

"In 2001, 2003, and 2004, I was so young that I didn't understand what this was all about and how challenging this is because everything happened so fast," Tom said.

He did now. It wasn't to be, though. Despite Tom completing sixteen consecutive passes at one point during the game and leading 17–15 late in the fourth, Eli again drove the Giants to a final-minute, Super Bowl–winning touchdown. It ended, New York winning 21–17.

Afterward, Tom spent a long time sitting silently

at his locker, unable to muster the physical or emotional energy to take his uniform off. While teammates showered, changed, and met with the media, Tom sat on a stool, hung his head, and stared at the space between his cleats. When he finally rose, he was in a daze of disappointment. It took so much work to get to this point. His first three trips ended in glory; the last two in a gut punch. He eventually cleaned up, got changed, spoke to reporters, and then walked out of Lucas Oil Stadium in Indianapolis holding Giselle's hand. For all that Tom Brady had going for him, for all that he had accomplished, there was still no disappointment quite like losing the Big Game.

"Those were challenging games," Tom said of the Super Bowl losses to the Giants. "They came down to the wire and we lost. I don't think those things discouraged me at all. They just reemphasized how hard and challenging it is to get to the Super Bowl and how challenging it is to win the game. I have such an appreciation for it now."

He also had no idea if he would ever get back.

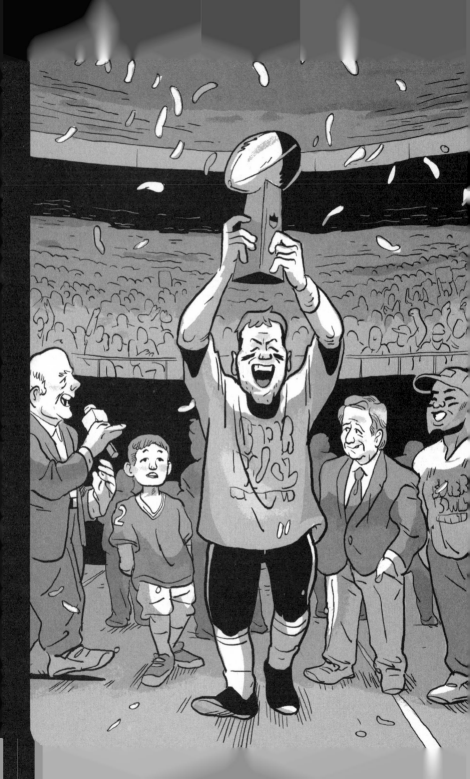

12

Redemption

IN BOTH 2012 AND 2013, the Patriots went 12–4 and won their opening playoff contest. Then, in each of those years they lost in the AFC Championship Game. First it was to Baltimore and then to Denver, which had signed Peyton Manning away from the Colts after Manning sat out a season with a neck injury. Peyton and Tom would play each other seventeen times, with Tom leading 11–6 overall, but Peyton winning three playoff games to Tom's two. The consistency and good seasons remained something to be proud of in New England. The failure to reach the ultimate—or by Patriots standards, the only—goal was frustrating.

As the years ticked by, the Patriots had to again revamp their offense. The Welker–Gronkowski–Hernandez offense became the Gronkowski–Julian Edelman–Danny Amendola offense. Tom just kept slinging it.

The 2014 season appeared to bring more of the same: another 12–4 regular season, another year of Tom putting up huge numbers (4,109 yards, thirty-three touchdowns) . . . and another playoff defeat. At least it looked that way when Baltimore led 28–14. Then Tom orchestrated a wild, second-half comeback to prevail 35–31.

The Patriots had been winning for so long that critics were waiting for them to collapse, constantly picking apart any mistake as a sign that Tom had lost it and the team would stumble. That season, New England had started 2–2, including a blowout loss at Kansas City. It was early in the season, but the doubters were out in force.

"We saw a weak team," analyst Trent Dilfer said on ESPN after the Kansas City loss. "The New England Patriots, let's face it, they're not good anymore." Inside Gillette Stadium, the quote just made players laugh but also work even harder. They promptly tallied eleven victories in thirteen games to get to their fourth consecutive AFC Championship Game. Then New England crushed Indianapolis 45–7 to advance to the Super Bowl. So much for "weak" and "not good anymore."

That AFC Championship Game became known as "Deflategate" after the Colts accused New England of playing with footballs in the first half that were slightly and intentionally deflated. The Colts claimed that allowed Tom to grip the ball better. The Patriots contended the minor deflation was just a natural reaction to cold air. Tom denied any wrongdoing or knowledge of it. He later sued the NFL to prove it, although he lost the case. He said he just played with the footballs he was given. Mostly, in the days after the accusation, he tried not to pay any attention.

"Coach always says, 'Ignore the noise and control what you can control,'" Tom said. In this case, it was preparing to win.

Their opponent would be formidable, the defending champion Seattle Seahawks. The game took place in Glendale, Arizona, where New England had suffered its most painful defeat, losing to the Giants when they were 18–0. Tom was zeroed in on winning, while still trying to appreciate that he was now in his sixth Super Bowl, tying him for the most appearances ever. Even after all these trips to the Big Game, he wanted to remember how rare it was and how fortunate he was. He tried to think back to when football was just a game to play without fans or television cameras watching his every move, without coaches or contracts.

"I loved having a chance as a kid to go out there and play with my friends," Tom said. "To play football in the street with the older boys was fun. To get a chance to play in the Super Bowl, I never thought I'd play in one. I never imagined this in my wildest dreams."

The Super Bowl against Seattle was everything fans hoped it would be, full of exciting plays and back-and-forth momentum swings. The Seahawks "Legion of Boom" defense was everything the Patriots had heard about. And Seattle's great quarterback Russell Wilson and powerhouse running back Marshawn Lynch were, too. Entering the fourth quarter, Seattle led 24–14. No team had ever come back from ten down in the final quarter and won a Super Bowl. The Pats weren't panicked, though. This is what Tom Brady does.

In this case, he went thirteen of fifteen for 124

yards, while leading two long drives that culminated in touchdown passes. In between, the New England defense held. Fans at home were both stunned and not surprised in the least—a Tom Brady comeback was practically expected by this point.

With 2:06 remaining, it was New England 28, Seattle 24. About the only mistake Tom made was not wasting more time off the clock before he scored. Seattle got the ball and began driving. They wound up on New England's five-yard line after receiver Jermaine Kearse made a circus catch. Standing on the sideline, Tom was in a panic. It felt just like the moments before the two Super Bowl losses to the Giants, a late drive crushing the Pats' hopes. That's when fate or fortune or just good football by New England stepped in. On first and goal, Seattle predictably ran the ball, handing it off to Marshawn Lynch, their huge running back whose rushing style is called "Beast Mode" since he's so ferocious. He was stopped on the one-yard line with 1:06 remaining, plenty of time for three more battering ram rushing attempts to get in and steal the win from the Patriots. It didn't seem possible New England's defense could stop him that many times just one yard away from the end zone.

Instead, Seattle had Wilson drop back to pass.

No one could believe it. Why? Why not give it to Marshawn? It seemed like a sure thing.

But Wilson threw a quick slant intended for Ricardo Lockette only to have New England rookie defensive back Malcolm Butler jam the route, knock Lockette back, and intercept the ball. Just like that, Seattle went from near-certain victory to blowing the game. It was one of the most unexpected plays in Super Bowl history. On the sideline, Tom jumped for joy, unable to imagine how, let alone why, it happened. The game was over a few plays later.

Tom was named the Super Bowl MVP for his stellar play. He was presented a fully loaded red Chevrolet Colorado pickup truck for being the MVP. But he quickly gave the keys to Butler as a gift. "He earned it," Tom said. "He deserved it. Without Malcolm, we don't win that game." Butler said he'll never sell the truck.

A fourth Super Bowl Championship tied Tom for the most of any quarterback, a list that included his boyhood idol Joe Montana. It also cemented the legacy of the Patriots, giving them a championship a decade after their previous one. And finally, it proved what Tom is always preaching.

Malcolm Butler's story was improbable. He grew

up poor in Vicksburg, Mississippi. He went to a community college and worked at Popeyes Louisiana Kitchen to pay the bills. He wound up at Division II University of West Alabama because no major schools were interested in him. When the 2014 NFL draft came, no one picked him. New England had scouted him and invited him to what they call a "rookie minicamp," basically a last-ditch tryout. Occasionally, a player will catch Belichick's eye and get invited to training camp. Malcolm did that. Even then, most of those players get cut before the season. Malcolm didn't. He made the team.

"He competed every day," Belichick said.

Just as he did with Tom, Belichick liked Malcolm's potential. He was the fifth defensive back on the team and mostly played a reserve role. Yet there he was on the critical play of the Super Bowl, where he took a look at the Seattle formation, recalled the scouting report, and jumped the route for one of the most dramatic plays in the history of the NFL. He didn't line up doubting he should be there with all these great players. He stepped up and proved he should.

This is how the Patriots win, by finding guys who prepare for a moment no one even knows for sure is coming. This is how Tom Brady became Tom Brady.

"Life is about taking advantage of opportunities," Tom said. "You never know when you're going to get them. You have to be prepared to take advantage when you get them. You try to go out there and be confident in yourself so you can inspire confidence in others. I always tell young players, 'How do you expect me to be confident in you when I look at you and see that you're not confident in yourself?'"

Two years later New England was back again, to take on Atlanta. (Remember that *unreal* comeback in chapter 1?) A season after that, in 2017, at age forty, long past when most quarterbacks retire, Brady threw for 4,577 yards and thirty-two touchdowns. He was named MVP for the third time. He was as good as ever. Better even, perhaps.

Consider the AFC Championship Game that season, which felt like a replay of the victory over Atlanta or the victory over Seattle. New England trailed Jacksonville 20–10 with 10:49 remaining in the game. The Jaguars defense was young and ferocious. Maybe this was it for the Pats. Then Tom Brady happened.

He passed to Danny Amendola for twenty-one yards. Then thirty-one to Phillip Dorsett. Then two more completions to Amendola, the last one a touchdown. Suddenly the once confident Jaguars felt the game slipping away, like they were starring in a horror movie they'd watched over and over growing up—a Tom Brady comeback.

New England got the ball back late in the fourth quarter and with Gillette Stadium rocking, it was more Brady. Fifteen yards to James White, a completion to Amendola, then another to Amendola, this time in the end zone to win the game. The exhausted Jags could only shake their heads and tip their hats.

"You can't give the Patriots any air," Jaguars' linebacker Myles Jack said. "If you get a pass interference, you get an offsides, they are going to capitalize on it. That's what makes them so great. Little things like that, the crowd gets into it, they start playing their song, Brady starts moving faster. It's pressure."

"The greatest quarterback of all time," Jaguars cornerback Jalen Ramsey added.

That meant a record eighth Super Bowl appearance for Tom, this time against the Philadelphia Eagles. He already owned a record five Super Bowl Championships and a record four Super Bowl MVP Awards.

This time he wouldn't deliver another championship to New England, although it was hardly his fault. Philly beat the Pats 41–33 mainly because the Eagles' offense was nearly unstoppable in the second half. In defeat, Tom threw for a Super Bowl record of 505 yards. He added three touchdowns. And he kept New England in it to the final play, an incomplete Hail Mary pass that just eluded the grasp of Gronk.

A year later, Tom would enter the 2018 season at forty-one years old, long past the typical retirement age for most payers. He was the oldest active quarterback in the NFL, and among only a handful of QBs in NFL history who had ever started a game after their forty-first birthday. No quarterback had ever won a Super Bowl past the age of thirty-eight. Yet as always, the Super Bowl was the only goal for Tom and New England. When the Patriots again started slow, including a low-energy loss to Detroit to bring their record to 1–2 on the season, the skeptics came out in full force.

Tom didn't flinch. Super Bowls aren't won in September, and the criticism fueled his work ethic. The team began to embrace a new rallying cry, "We're still here," to fend off all the critics and commentators who were writing them off and instead turning their attention to exciting, young teams such as the Kansas City Chiefs and Los Angeles Rams. He began posting Instagram messages with the phrase to rally fans and teammates and remind everyone that the Patriots hadn't gone anywhere yet.

New England took that statement to heart and finished 11–5, winning the AFC East division for a record tenth consecutive season. It was the Pats' sixteenth playoff appearance in the seventeen seasons Tom was a healthy starter.

In the first round of the playoffs, New England easily dispatched the Los Angeles Chargers to set up an AFC Championship showdown in Kansas City against the Chiefs and their dynamic, second-year quarterback, Patrick Mahomes. Mahomes was just twenty-three years old and would be named NFL MVP that season. Many saw this as a potential changing of the guard, the great old star against a great new one. Tom no longer put up league-leading stats or was a contender for MVP. It didn't mean he wasn't great, and it certainly didn't mean he was ready to be pushed aside quite yet.

On that cold night in Kansas City, he looked as good as ever, throwing for 348 yards and leading the

Pats to three touchdown drives in the fourth quarter and overtime. It was enough to win 37–31 and advance the Pats to Tom's record ninth Super Bowl.

After the game, Tom asked a security guard to take him into the Chiefs' locker room so he could personally congratulate Mahomes on a great season and wish him well. He knew Mahomes was hurting from the loss and wanted to lift his spirits with some sportsmanship. "He's a great player," Tom said.

This was New England's third consecutive Super Bowl appearance and fourth in five years. The Los Angeles Rams were their opponent, making their first appearance since 2002 . . . when the franchise was located in St. Louis and they'd lost to a rookie QB named Tom Brady. Tom was particularly comfortable in the spotlight; experience had taught him how to handle the pressure and get ready to face an opposing defense.

As much he prepared, though, the Rams' defense proved particularly tough in the game, and Tom was not as sharp as usual. The score was tied 3–3 after three quarters. Some years, New England had the most talented team in the NFL. This was not one of those years. They had skill and experience, but they needed to grind out victories.

Tenacity would win the day. In the fourth quarter, Tom took a deep breath, relaxed, and began to play his game. He may have struggled with some of his throws earlier on, but on a critical, late drive, he feathered a beautiful twenty-nine-yard pass to Gronk to set up New England's only score—a two-yard run by Sony Michel. Thanks to the Pats' great defense, it would prove to be enough—they went on to win, 13–3.

"We fought through it more than anything," Tom said following the victory. "It's unbelievable to win this game."

Tom had won his sixth Super Bowl, more than any player in NFL history. When he was presented the trophy, he held it aloft in one hand while holding his six-year-old daughter, Vivian, in the other. Confetti fell all around them. It was, again, a magical moment.

And it was a testament to a player who never gave up or listened too closely when his doubters aired their opinions. Not when they said he'd never be as skilled as his older sisters. Not when his path was uncertain at Michigan. Not when he went late in the draft. Not early in his career against Oakland or Saint Louis or Indianapolis. Not late in his career against Seattle or Jacksonville. Not when he was told he was too old.

Not even against Atlanta, when he was flat out on the field, watching his pick-six get returned or when he looked at a scoreboard that read Falcons 28, Patriots 3. Instead he walked those sidelines and shouted encouragement at those young players and demanded they seize the opportunity in front of them.

They listened, of course, and came roaring back to win. It was Tom Brady talking to them, after all.

Instant
Replay

ALFORD RETURNS THE INTERCEPTION FOR A TOUCHDOWN, GIVING THE FALCONS A TWENTY-POINT LEAD.
NE ATL
0 20
2nd 2:21
BRADY
12

NE | ATL
9 | 28
4th | 12:18
3rd & 1

NE | ATL
12 | 28
4th | 9:44

FIELD
GOAL

THE PATRIOTS' COMEBACK
CONTINUES WITH A FIELD
GOAL TO BRING THEM
WITHIN TWO TOUCHDOWNS.

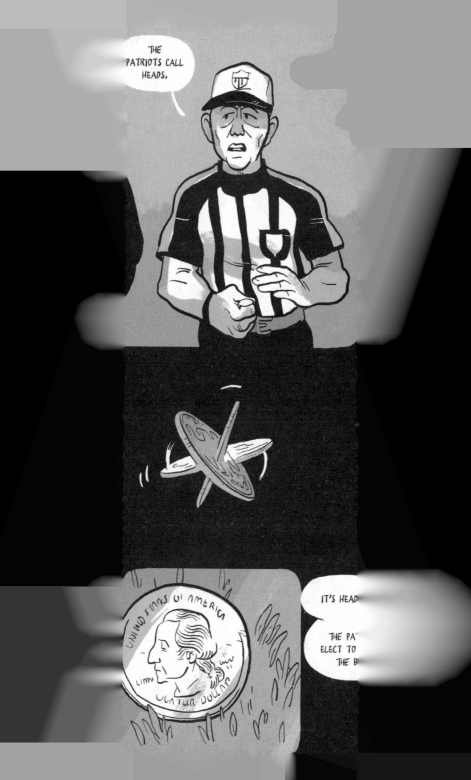

NE 28 ATL 28
OT 11:56
1st & 10

TOM LOBS THE BALL TO JAMES WHITE, WHO TAKES IT TO THE FALCONS' FIFTEEN-YARD LINE.

The Nonstop Sports Action Continues!

Here's an excerpt of
EPIC ATHLETES
STEPHEN CURRY

1

Underdog

Twenty thousand Cleveland Cavaliers fans stood inside Quicken Loans Arena and tried to distract Stephen Curry. They stomped their feet. They waved their arms. They cupped their hands up to their faces and screamed.

It was Game 6 of the 2015 NBA Finals, and Cleveland's J. R. Smith had just drained a three-pointer. A Golden State lead that only minutes before had stretched to thirteen points was now just four, 101–97. There were 29.0 seconds remaining, still enough time for the Cavaliers to mount a comeback. Golden State led the series 3–2 and was trying to win the franchise's first NBA title in forty years. The Warriors wanted to end the series right then, in this game, and avoid having to play a decisive Game 7. They didn't want to give Cleveland superstar LeBron James another chance to win it all.

Cleveland had all the momentum. It was up to Curry to stop it, win the game, and grab the championship that he had spent a lifetime dreaming about.

Golden State had won sixty-seven games in the regular season, among the most by any team in NBA history. Behind Curry and teammate Klay Thompson, dubbed the "Splash Brothers" for the way so many of their long three-pointers splashed through the net, the team had cruised to The Finals with a 12–3 record. It was expected to beat Cleveland handily, especially after one of the Cavs' stars, Kyrie Irving, was lost to injury.

Instead, LeBron raised his level of play and Cleveland took two of the first three games. To make matters worse, Steph, the best player in the league that season, was in a slump. His usually reliable shot was off. At the end of the Game 2 loss, he shot just two of fifteen from three-point range. He even tossed up an air ball, missing the rim altogether. "Shots I normally make . . . I knew as soon as they left my hand that they were off," Steph explained. "That doesn't usually happen."

In the media, there was talk that Steph wasn't tough enough for the big games and the pressure of the NBA Finals was getting to him. He had shaken that off and returned to form in Games 4, 5, and now Game 6. The Warriors clawed back and took the lead in the series. They couldn't imagine it all coming undone in the last minute.

Everything rested on the slim shoulders of Steph Curry, who had been fouled and awarded two free throws. If he missed one or both of the shots from the line, Cleveland still had a chance. If he hit them, Golden State was almost assuredly going to win.

With the pressure mounting and the noise of all those Cavaliers fans raining down on him, Steph walked to the free-throw line. For years he had dreamed of and practiced for this moment. His entire life he'd been told over and over the same thing by coaches, scouts, and the media—that he would never be good enough to be a great college star or NBA player, let alone the MVP of the entire league.

Too small, they said. Too short, they claimed. Too little, they argued.

Curry now stood six foot three and weighed 190 pounds. That was small by NBA standards. LeBron, for instance, checked in at six-eight and 265 pounds of muscle. Curry had always been undersized, though, and he adapted his game around that fact. He was sometimes the smallest kid on the court in middle school. As a high school sophomore, he said he was "a little scrawny kid, like maybe five foot six, five foot seven and 120 pounds." So he learned to shoot the ball with a high arc to avoid the outstretched arms of taller kids who would try to block his shot. By using quick dribbles and his speed, he found ways to create space on the court to get the ball up in the air and away from bigger players attempting to steal it from him.

He also knew that if there was one place on a basketball court where his height and weight didn't matter, it was the free-throw line. No one is allowed to guard you there. No one can stop you from hitting every shot you take. The free-throw line doesn't care who you are. It's just you, the ball, and the rim, fifteen feet away, ten feet in the air. In a sport with so much movement, it is the one time everything is the same, from grade school basketball to here in the NBA Finals. It's the one time the game stands still—but the pressure is still impossible to ignore.

Steph couldn't count the hours he'd spent perfecting his routine and shot from the line. He was never going to be a great dunker. He was never going to be able to muscle over opponents and score easily. He understood his strengths and didn't complain about his weaknesses. He knew he had to take points where he could get them. Besides, if bigger players were going to test his toughness and foul him, if they were going to attempt to bully him, the best revenge was to make both free throws. Eventually they'd stop or lose the game.

It started back in the driveway of his family's home in Charlotte, North Carolina. It continued through his days at Charlotte Christian School and then Davidson College, the small school that believed in his potential. It remained a daily habit across his first six years in the NBA, when many wondered if he'd ever become a star.

No matter how good Curry got, he never stopped working on the basics, and that meant free throws. The key to hitting free throws is using the exact same approach and technique on every shot, even before you release the ball. It was a lesson his father, Dell, taught him at an early age. If you are dedicated to your training, then you always have something to lean back on.

Hungry for More EPIC ATHLETES? Look Out for These Superstar Biographies, in Stores Now!

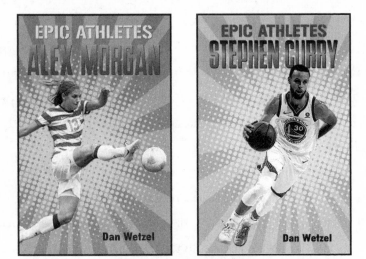

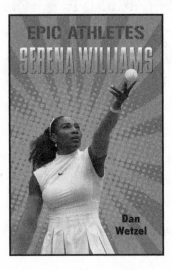